"Beautiful and good things":
The Dress of Anaïs Nin
1931-1932

"Beautiful and good things":

The Dress of Anaïs Nin 1931-1932

Gwendolyn M. Michel

"Beautiful and good things": The Dress of Anaïs Nin, 1931-1932

Copyright © Gwendolyn M. Michel, 2018. All rights reserved.

Publisher's Note: This book is a reproduction of the content of a doctoral dissertation submitted to Iowa State University, Ames, Iowa, United States of America in partial fulfillment of the requirements for the degree of Doctor of Philosophy in Apparel, Merchandising, and Design, published with permission of the author and copyright holder, Gwendolyn M. Michel.
The contents can also be retrieved from the Iowa State University Digital Repository
Graduate Theses and Dissertations Number 17268
https://lib.dr.iastate.edu/etd/17268

Published by Reflective Ink Press
P.O. Box 178
Moss Landing, CA 95039
www.reflectiveinkpress.com

ISBN: 978-0-9991222-3-5
Printed in the United States of America

Contents

Acknowledgments	i
Abstract	iii
Chapter 1	
Introduction	1
Overview	1
Purpose Statement	3
Theoretical Approach and Positionality of the Researcher	3
Method	3
Rationale for the Study	3
Significance	4
Research Question	5
Assumptions and Limitations of Study	5
Organization of the Dissertation	6
Definition of Terms	6
Chapter 2	
Literature Review	9
Overview	9
Biographical History	9
Previous Literature on the Dress of Anaïs Nin	12
Cultural Context: Nin's Interwar Paris	14
The Use of Autobiography and Diaries as Source Material in Dress Studies	17
Chapter 3	
Method	19

Overview	19
Method of Data Collection	19
The Author(s) and Editors of Henry and June	24
Primary Sources Utilized in the Study	31
Diary 33 and Diary 33 Bis	33
Method of Data Analysis	35
Reliability and Validity	36

Chapter 4
Results

	39
Overview	39
Overview of Nin's Dress and Appearance Practices: 1931-1932	40
Nin's Dress for Day	43
The Millers Come to Dinner: June Miller's Appearance as Related to Nin's	45
Stockings	53
Shoes	56
Cosmetics: Lip Rouge, Powder, and Nail Polish	57
Nin's Make-up	58
Nail Polish	60
June Miller's Make-up	61
Perfume	62
The Scent of the Diaries	68
Hairstyling	70
Jewelry	72
Undergarments	77
Evening Dresses	79
Outerwear: Capes, Coats, and Jackets	83
Hats and Turbans	86

Other Accessories	87
Sleepwear and Loungewear	88
Cosmetic Surgery	88
Spanish Dance Costume	91
Body Image	93
The Effects of Henry Miller's Appraisal of Nin's Appearance	96
Nin's Abiding Love of Luxury within A Bourgeois-Bohemian Tension	100 |//

Chapter 5
Discussion and Conclusions — 111

Overview	111
"Beautiful and good things"	111
Tseëlon's Paradox Three: The Visibility Paradox	113
Implications: Composing a Text, Composing a Self	124
Limitations	126
Suggestions for Future Study	126
Conclusions	127

References — 129

Acknowledgments

Simple thanks will never be enough to express how appreciated and valued are all those who supported this endeavor. First and foremost, I would like to thank my committee chair, Sara Marcketti, and my committee members, Mary Lynn Damhorst, Eulanda Sanders, Michèle Schaal, and Christiana Langenberg, for their guidance and support throughout the course of this research. To Dr. Marcketti and Dr. Damhorst, thank you for our years of collaboration. Here's to many more. To Dr. Sanders, it was your research on narrative that inspired this study in its earliest form. To my outside committee members, Dr. Schaal and Christiana Langenberg, thank you to both of you for recommending so many good books which served to inspire and shape this study. To each of my committee members, my deepest gratitude and warmest appreciation for your time, suggestions, expertise, and patient shepherding as I made the journey from proposal to completion.

Much of this study's data collection was supported by a Stella Blum Student Research Grant from the Costume Society of America. To the Costume Society of America and the late Stella Blum, my sincere thanks and appreciation. I want to also offer my appreciation to Paul Herron of Sky Blue Press, Tree Wright of the Anaïs Nin Literary Trust, and the staff of the departments of special collections at the University of California, Los Angeles and University of San Francisco libraries for their assistance and support. Special thanks go to John Hawk at the University of San Francisco's Gleeson Library. Lastly, for those who provided lifelong support to Anaïs Nin, an appreciation: Hugh P. Guiler and Rupert Pole.

Abstract

Anaïs Nin (b: 1903, d: 1977) was a twentieth-century author of fiction and a lifelong diary. She was born in France, raised in Belgium, Spain, and New York, and spent her adult life in France, New York, and California. Nin's published diaries were the work that brought her the most recognition in life. In 1986, the first of a series of posthumously published unexpurgated diaries revealed Nin's romantic partnership with American author Henry Miller (b: 1891, d: 1980) and a short-lived intimate relationship with her cousin Eduardo Sanchez (b: 1904, d: 1986). Using the historical research method, this study documented Nin's dress and appearance practices, as described in the diaries, in 1931-1932. This study examined the original, handwritten journals upon which the first volume of Nin's unexpurgated published diaries was based, specifically those written October 1931 through October 1932, plus the journal of Nin's husband, Hugh P. Guiler (b: 1898, d: 1985), and related secondary sources.

This study's findings included Nin's overall appearance, apparel (including dress for day and evening), cosmetic surgery, Spanish dance costume, body image, the effects of Henry Miller's appraisal of her appearance, and a love of luxury that existed within a bourgeois-bohemian tension. Nin loved silk stockings and French perfume, felt her self-esteem enhanced by

Henry Miller's admiration of her appearance, and had an awareness of her appearance and its effects on herself and others. She was aware of Henry Miller's fascination with slum living and her own fascination with his wife June Mansfield Miller's (b: 1902, d: 1979) bohemian ways. Although Nin spent many days and nights in Henry Miller's apartment in Paris, she was never to give up her bourgeois life with her husband Hugh P. Guiler (not even after her bigamous 1955 marriage to Rupert Pole, b: 1919, d: 2006). She may have sacrificed on her dress in some respects, by wearing mended stockings to save to be able to spend money on gifts for Henry Miller, but she also made cosmetic surgery a priority. As Nin herself wrote, "Absolute luxury is not a necessity to me, but beautiful and good things are."

Chapter 1
Introduction

Overview

Society girl, artist's model, Spanish dancer, banker's wife, and author: Anaïs Nin (b:1903, d: 1977), a French-born woman of Danish-French and Cuban-Spanish ancestry, called herself each of these during her life. Anaïs Nin was all of these things, and more. By her death in Los Angeles in January 1977, Nin's published body of work included six volumes of *The Diary of Anaïs Nin* (cf., Nin, 1966, 1967, & 1969), a book of literary criticism (Nin, 1932), a prose poem (Nin, 1936), a collection of novellas (Nin, 1939), six novels (cf., Nin, 1959/1987), and essays (cf., Nin, 1968 & 1976). Until the publication of the first volume of *The Diary of Anaïs Nin (1931-1934)* (Nin, 1966), Nin struggled to find an audience for her work, which was predominantly surrealistic fiction focused on women's inner psychological experiences (cf., Nin, 1939). It was not until 1966 that Nin would see her first significant professional recognition.

The Diary of Anaïs Nin: 1931-1934 (Nin, 1966) was followed by more than a dozen volumes, the result of a lifelong diary practice. The diaries became a window into the inner experience of a twentieth-century woman who emigrated from Europe to the United States at the age of eleven, moved among the avant-garde literary circles of 1930s Paris and 1940s New York, and led a bi-coastal life split between New York and California during the last thirty years of her life (Bair, 1995; Fitch, 1993; Nin, 2017).

This dissertation focuses on the dress of Anaïs Nin, particularly her subjective experience of the embodied performance of femininity as described in her handwritten journals. These journal entries were the source material for the posthumously published, unexpurgated edition of her journals dated 1931-1932: *Henry and June, from a Journal of Love: The Unexpurgated Diary of Anaïs Nin, 1931-1932* (Nin, 1986). The book was published after Nin's death and the first in the unexpurgated series of Nin's diaries (cf., Nin, 1992, 1995, & 2017). Composed mainly of previously unpublished excerpts from Nin's handwritten diaries of the period, with some material from Nin (1966), *Henry and June* (Nin, 1986), was prepared and edited by Harcourt Brace Jovanovich editor John Ferrone (b: 1924, d: 2017) with significant input from Nin's second husband, Rupert Pole (b: 1919, d: 2006) (Bair, 1995; Pole & Ferrone, 2007). More information on that editorial process is presented in Chapter 3.

This study examined Nin's life at the ages of 28 and 29, when the French-born writer lived with her husband, mother, and brother in Louveciennes, a suburb of Paris. The decision to focus on the *Henry and June* (Nin, 1986) period in this dissertation was based on several turning points in Nin's life and writing. When Nin published the first volume of her journals (Nin, 1966), she began with her journal entries from the autumn of 1931, a decision that was reflective of her developing voice as a writer and the historical significance of that period in history and Nin's personal life. In late 1931, Nin's first book, *D. H. Lawrence: An Unprofessional Study* (Nin, 1932), had just been accepted for publication. In December 1931, Nin met American writer Henry Miller (b: 1891, d: 1980) and his wife June Mansfield Miller (b: 1902, d: 1979). Compared to her writings in the 1920s, Nin had begun to discuss in late 1930 and in 1931 more candidly her interests in sexuality and psychoanalysis (cf., Nin, 1985). This intensified, including personal examination of the meaning behind her style of dress and appearance as she met the Millers in 1931, and entered psychoanalysis in 1932. Nin lived an upper-middle class life in which she explored her love of creativity in life and beautiful things, which were in turn reflected in her dress and its description in her journals. In her journals, Nin described her experiences in a way that made reality as appealing as fiction. Nin used dress as a means for costuming herself as she moved through life, acting at various times as a bourgeois banker's wife, Spanish dancer, surrealist writer, artist's model, and muse to artists, authors and revolutionaries. Nin often wrote of the role dress played in her life: as art, as costume in playing various personae in everyday life, as dance costume, and even, referring to her lies as costumes. Until now, Nin's dress has not been fully explored by scholars.

This study examined the handwritten diary entries on which the 1986 book was based.

Purpose Statement

The purpose of this historical study was to discover Anaïs Nin's expression of her dress and appearance, as communicated in her handwritten journals from October 1931 through October 1932, which were the source material for the unexpurgated edition of those journals, *Henry and June* (Nin, 1986).

Theoretical Approach and Positionality of the Researcher

As a qualitative study, this work acknowledges the role of the researcher as the instrument for data collection and the influence of the subjective position of the author upon the findings of the study. This study took the ontological position that, in the context of intimate, personal writings such as diaries, the nature of reality is whatever a diarist perceives it to be. Anaïs Nin gave words to her lived experiences in her journals, and those are the words this study has examined to produce its findings.

Method

This study examined both primary and secondary sources, namely Nin's handwritten diaries, that of her first husband, Hugh P. Guiler, and biographical texts about the Guilers (Anaïs Nin and Hugh) and the Millers (Henry and June). Methods of triangulation among these various sources and having my major professor review my data, drafts, and writings of Nin, were also employed. Method is discussed in detail in Chapter Three.

Rationale for the Study

Anaïs Nin received much attention for her published diaries in the 1960s and 1970s (e.g., Nin, 1966). In the 1980s and 1990s, the so-called "unexpurgated" editions of her diaries, posthumously published, and two salacious biographies in the 1990s (Bair 1995; Fitch, 1993) brought her infamy. Although Nin wrote and published fiction before she published her diaries, it is her diaries that continue to number the most pages in print and for which she has received the most attention from scholars.

The literature within Nin studies and the memoirs of those who knew her contain numerous reflections on the elegance of Nin's dress (i.e., Franklin, 1996; Herron, 1996; Raphael, 2003; Kraft, 2013). However, few scholars have focused on Nin's dress exclusively. Notable exceptions include: an unpublished conference presentation by dress scholar Tove Hermanson (2010), a short paper by Nin scholar and screenwriter Kim Krizan (2011). Krizan (2011)'s paper, not peer-reviewed, focused on Nin's writings on dress as recorded in her published diaries kept from ages 11 to 17 (Nin, 1978). This study is a unique contribution in that it exhaustively examines Nin's dress and subjective experience as reflected in just one 12-month period in her life, by examining primary sources, namely Nin's handwritten diaries.

Significance

This study is of significance due to Nin's status as a twentieth-century author who made significant contributions to women's literature and life-writing, and to Nin studies, in particular, because no scholar has composed an in-depth study of Nin's dress from a perspective of dress history to date. This study's findings expand understanding of Nin's life and her creative uses of dress, adding to the literature in Nin and dress studies, respectively. Through the use of diaries, the present study underscores the value of personal diaries as a resource for dress, literary, and cultural historians. The timeless elegance and attention to detail which characterized Nin's personal style have been commented on in numerous recollections of those who knew her in life (cf., Franklin, 1996; Herron, 1996; Kraft, 2013). The published editions of Nin's diaries contain her thoughts and perspectives on dress, and the original, handwritten diaries in the University of California, Los Angeles's (UCLA) library, available to the public for examination, revealed yet more of Nin's words on dress. Perhaps Nin has been overlooked by dress scholars because her personal reputation seemed to have been damaged in the 1990s by the publication of two biographies (Bair, 1995; Fitch, 1993) and the publication of the unexpurgated editions of her journals in the 1990s (Nin, 1992, in particular). For example, Nin's (1992) unexpurgated diary, *Incest*, described in detail a short-lived incestuous affair with her father and revealed the stillbirth described in Nin (1966) was actually a late-term abortion. Since the publication of Bair (1995), Nin scholars have blamed Bair's (1995) overly moralistic description for Nin's decline in popularity. True, Nin conducted many romantic and sexual affairs at that time (and in the decade to follow), but as one author notes, the Bair biography was written at a time when "Crucially, the word 'slut-shaming' simply did not exist" (Doyle, 2015, para. 31). Further, this study found several discrepancies between Bair (1995) and Nin (1986) and the diaries in UCLA holdings, as explained in Chapters 3 and 4. Further, Nin (1986) is closer to an autobiographical novel, as explained in Chapter 3. Although literary scholars have touched on dress in works of literature, such as novels, this has been done less so by dress scholars (Hughes, 2005; McNeil, Karaminas, & Cole 2009). Clair Hughes (2005) wrote that "costume historians have frequently drawn on literature for evidence and information" (Hughes, 2005, p. 2), but autobiographical texts and novels appear to be underutilized by dress historians at present. This study is significant in that it examined autobiographical text from the perspective of dress history and because it is a study of an historical figure that has not received extensive attention of dress historians. The use of the historical method (Fitzpatrick, 2007) is discussed in detail in Chapter 3.

Research Question

- What was Nin's subjective experience of dress and appearance as described in her handwritten journals from October 1931-October 1932?

Assumptions and Limitations of Study

This study focused on a one-year period in Nin's life as written about in her diaries that inspired the published work, *Henry and June, from A Journal of Love: The Unexpurgated Diary of Anaïs Nin, 1931-1932* (Nin, 1986). This study examined Nin's handwritten journals from October 1931 – October 1932, the journals which were the source of the material which became Nin (1986). The rationale behind the decision to examine the handwritten diaries, rather than the published work of *Henry and June* (1986) is explained in detail in Chapter 3. Few photographs were examined for this study; those that were glued into the diaries were either of Henry Miller, or his wife, June Miller, not of Nin. Photographs of Nin from the Anaïs Nin Trust were used to provide evidence of some of the information Nin wrote about. However, a detailed analysis of the photographs or comparison of the photographs was not completed due to the limited number of available photographs dated 1931-1932.

Organization of the Dissertation

This dissertation is composed of five chapters: Chapter 1 introduces the study's topic, purpose, theoretical approach and positionality of the researcher, method, rationale, significance, research question, assumptions and limitations, organization of the dissertation, and definition of terms. Chapter 2 provides a biographical background, cultural and historical context, and review of relevant literature from Nin studies and dress studies. Chapter 3 explains the historical research method used in this study. Chapter 4 presents the study's findings. Chapter 5 summarizes and provides the conclusion to the study.

Definition of Terms

Appearance: A larger construct than dress (defined below), in that it also includes "facial expressions, costume, adornment, or mannerisms" (Hillestad, 1980, p. 117). Appearance includes the body, which may be shaped by "prevailing attitudes toward nutrition, grooming, and concepts of ideal beauty" and body motions, such as posture (Hillestad, 1980, p. 121). Hillestad (1980) noted appearance engages the senses of sight and touch, and can also engage the sense of smell with the use of "cosmetics, perfumes, and other scented substances" (Hillestad, 1980, p. 117). To expand on Hillestad's (1980) sensual perception of appearance, it is only for the sighted that appearance engages the sense of sight, while appearance potentially engages the sense of touch both on the part of the one who is appearing and those who interact with that person. To closely follow scent, appearance can also engage the sense of taste (consider jewelry made of candy beads, for example). I would argue appearance's potential sense engagement should also include the sense of hearing, with the use of clothing and accessories that generate sound, either incidentally (squeaking shoes, for example) or intentionally (i.e., wearing bells attached to clothing or as standalone adornment).

Autobiography: Autobiography is generally defined as retrospective, non-fiction, first-person, narrative in which the narrator and author are one and the same and the text is principally about the author (Kadar, 1992; Lejeune, 1989).

Diary/journal: Anaïs Nin, in her handwritten diary/journals dating from the years that this study covers (1931-1932), referred to her works as *journals*; later, when published, they were titled or sub-titled *The Diary of Anaïs Nin* (Nin, 1966 & 1986). Like other works on diaries and journals (Lejeune, 2009; Mallon,

1984; Nussbaum, 1988; Podnieks, 2000), this study used the terms *diary* and *journal* interchangeably. This literary form is one that is "written [in] the moment rather than from a retrospective...stance" (Nussbaum, 1988, p. 128), "discontinuous, full of gaps...redundant and repetitive" (Lejeune, 2009, p. 170). Unlike a retrospective autobiography, a journal, with its relative present-tense in the life of the author, the reading of a diary can invoke a sense of "...immediacy, the sense of being involved in an actual life in process...A diary seems to be real life going on..." (Blodgett, 1996, p. 156). The Finding Aid from UCLA's Charles E. Young Research Library's Department of Special Collections refers to them as diaries, although Nin herself seemed to have preferred the word "journal" (further, in print, the journals of her lifetime, as an *oeuvre*, were sometimes referred to as "the diary"). This study uses the words diary and journal interchangeably, except when citing Nin's journals in the UCLA library: those are cited as they are inventoried in the Finding Aid, for simplification in aiding future scholars and verification of this study's findings.

Dress: This study used dress scholar Hillestad's (1980) definition of *dress* as "the result of assembling various articles about the body [including]...[a]rticles of clothing and articles of adornment" (Hillestad, 1980, pp. 117-118). To briefly define those two terms, clothing and adornment, as subsets of the term dress:

> Gowns, shirts, trousers, and coats are but a few examples of articles generally classified as clothing. Jewelry, cosmetics and certain grooming aids are articles which are usually referred to as adornment. (Hillestad, 1980, p. 118)

Similarly, whereas Hillestad (1980) used the terms clothing and adornment, dress scholars Roach-Higgins and Eicher (1992) used the terms "modifications" and "supplements," to define dress thusly:

> ...direct modifications of the body, such as coiffed hair, colored skin, pierced ears, and scented breath, as well as an equally long list of garments, jewelry, accessories, and other categories of items added to the body as supplements. (Roach-Higgins & Eicher, 1992, p. 1)

Building on the definitions above, examples of dress practices include the acts of dressing, shopping for clothing and articles of adornment, caring for, altering, and repairing clothing, and plastic surgery.

Chapter 2
Literature Review

Overview

his chapter begins with a biographical background of Anaïs Nin, reviews relevant literature from Nin studies, provides a cultural and historical context, and reviews relevant literature from dress studies.

Biographical History

The daughter of the Cuban-Spanish composer and pianist Joaquín Nin y Castellanos and Cuban-Danish-French singer Rosa Culmell, Nin was raised in various European cities until the age of 11, when her parents separated. In 1914, Nin emigrated from Barcelona to New York with her mother and two younger brothers and it was on this voyage that she began her lifelong practice of diary keeping. From the very beginning, Nin's observations and reflections on her life included the role that dress played in her everyday life (Krizan, 2011; Nin, 1978).

Rosa Culmell Nin settled with her children in New York to be near her sisters. Anaïs Nin's large, extended family included many Cuban-Danish-French aunts, uncles and cousins, and given her parents' musical background, Nin was part of an international family and community that included many musicians. In her late teens in the early 1920s, Nin attended school and parties, modeled for artists and Seventh Avenue manufacturers, and described her dress for these activities in her journals (Bair, 1995, pp. 54 & 61; Fitch, 1993, pp. 45-47; Nin, 1982). As the eldest child of a single mother, Nin assisted with her mother's personal shopping and import/export business which bought fabric and clothing in New York City for wealthy women in Cuba. Nin wrote often of the hand-me-downs she received from her wealthy Cuban cousins. Nin was also a lover of books and was ever-curious about philosophy and her place in the world; she read Carlyle's *Sartor Resartus* and Ibsen's *A Doll's House* at this time, reflecting on both in her journal (Nin, 1982). When the Nin household ran into financial hard times, Anaïs Nin turned to modeling and registered with the Art Worker's Club for Women, an artists' models' guild in New York City, to find work (Fitch, 1993, p. 44). As Fitch described, it was "her first job, a short-lived (perhaps 8-month) career modeling for artists, illustrators, and photographers" (1993, p. 44). Nin's modeling was primarily as "an artist's character model, in other words, fully clothed, work her artistic European family found quite respectable" (Duxler, 2002, p. 37), and she would borrow various costumes from the lending wardrobe at the Art Worker's Club for her modeling work (Nin, 1982). During this modeling, Nin modeled for Charles Dana Gibson (after which she referred to herself as having been a "Gibson Girl"), Luis Mora, Neysa McMein, and others, and graced the July 8, 1922 cover of the *Saturday Evening Post* (Fitch, 1993, p. 45; Nin, 1982, pp. 411 & 414).

In addition to working as an artists' model, Nin modeled ready-to-wear for Jaeckel's in New York City until she was sent by her mother to stay with family in Havana, Cuba, and have her coming out into Havana society (Fitch, 1993, p. 45; Nin, 1982, pp. 411 & 414). Not long after her arrival in Havana, Nin was joined by her beau from New York, Scottish-American Hugh Parker Guiler (b: 1898, d: 1985), later known as the engraver and experimental filmmaker Ian Hugo. The two married and returned to New York shortly thereafter, for Hugh Guiler had agreed to support not only his new bride, but his mother-in-law and Nin's two brothers, Thorvald and Joaquín, as well. Nin's youngest brother, known as Joaquín Nin-Culmell to differentiate himself from their father, had inherited his father's talent for piano and composing. When Joaquín was admitted to the prestigious *Schola Cantorum* in Paris after high school, Guiler requested a transfer to his employer's Paris branch. Rosa and Joaquín moved to Paris in August 1924 for the start of the new school year; in late December, the Guilers followed. Living in Paris, the Guiler and Nin family remained part of an international community of musicians and artists.

After the move to Paris, Hugh Guiler began to achieve financial success and Nin settled into her role as bourgeois banker's wife. The Guilers were to live in Paris and its suburb, Louveciennes, from 1924 to 1939, interspersed with frequent travel for Hugh Guiler's work and for vacations. This period was to prove crucial for Nin's development as an adult and as a writer. During this time, Nin experimented with different forms of fiction, essays, and journal writing, continued to model for artists, became an amateur Spanish dancer, and published a book of essays on British author D. H. Lawrence's fictional treatment of women's sexuality (Nin, 1932) and two books of surrealistic fiction (Nin, 1936 & Nin, 1939). Active in Paris's Cuban community in Paris since their arrival, the joint Guiler and Nin household participated regularly in social events, teas, and dances, including piano performances by Nin's brother Joaquín Nin-Culmell and dance performances by Nin and Hugh Guiler. After first living in Montparnasse, the family moved in 1929 to adjacent and stylish apartments in Paris, near the Bois de Boulogne (Nin, 1985). Nin was a young, married, upper-middle class, writer who, along with her family, cultivated the company of artists, writers, and musicians. In early 1930, Nin had two main creative outlets, Spanish dance and writing, and hoped to use both to add to the household income (Nin, 1985). After a busy performance season, however, her health began to suffer, and she withdrew from dancing (Nin, 1985). Long a writer of fiction and her journal, Nin began to focus heavily on writing as a means for an income (Nin, 1985). Discovery of the writings of D. H. Lawrence, Sigmund Freud, and Carl Jung in the late 1920s and early 1930s led to Nin's interest in women's psychological experiences and sexuality, topics her journals reflect (Nin, 1966, 1985, & 1986). Due to the 1929 stock market crash, the combined Guiler-Nin family moved to a large house in Louveciennes, a suburb of Paris, to economize in late 1930. In Louveciennes, Nin wrote her first published book, *D. H. Lawrence: An Unprofessional Study* (Nin, 1932).

When Nin met Henry Miller in late 1931, it was a meeting that sparked a passionate relationship between the two then-unknown writers. Meeting Miller's wife, June Mansfield Miller, shortly thereafter sparked a romantic flirtation between the two women, leading to an intense infatuation on Nin's part (Nin, 1966 & 1986). Obsessed with June Miller, Nin formed a literary friendship and alliance with Henry Miller. By March 1932, Nin and Henry Miller had begun a romantic affair that was to last into the 1940s and sparked a rich period in each author's writing. Nin financed the publication of Miller's first book, *Tropic of Cancer* (Miller, 1934/1961; see also Dearborn, 1991, p. 171;

Jong, 1994, p. 116) and was even known to inflate her dressmaker's bills to support Miller financially (Kraft, 2016). In the early 1930s, Nin not only had a dalliance with June Miller and a partnership with Henry Miller, she also had longer term sexual and romantic affairs with her cousin Eduardo Sanchez (b:1904, d:1986) and her psychoanalyst Dr. René Allendy (Bair, 1995; Fitch, 1993). In the context of her psychoanalytic sessions with Dr. Allendy, Nin discussed her need for distinctive dress, which she sometimes referred to as "costumes" in everyday life, while also referring to lies she told as "costumes:"

> I see myself wrapped in lies, which do not seem to penetrate my soul, as if they are not really a part of me. They are like costumes. When I loved Henry, as I did those four days, I loved him with a naked body that had shed its costumes and forgotten its lies. (Nin, 1986, p. 231).

Previous Literature on the Dress of Anaïs Nin

The literature within Nin studies and the memoirs of those who knew her contain numerous mentions on the elegance of Nin's dress and appearance by those who knew her, but only towards the end of her life, after she had achieved fame for her published diaries (i.e., DuBow, 1994; Franklin, 1996; Herron, 1996; Kraft, 2013; Raphael, 2003). Time and time again, Nin was described as having a delicate, feminine bearing and an almost magical presence. In the words of Maryanne Raphael, a friend of Nin's in the 1970s:

> I'll never forget the first time I met her...She was the most beautiful woman I'd ever seen. With high cheekbones, flawless skin, bright brown eyes and hair pulled into a bun, her Greta Garbo beauty took my breath away. Dressed in an aquamarine, velvet, floor-length gown that accentuated her firm and slender body, her presence gave forth an aura of mystery. It was hard to believe she was almost seventy. With a dancer's walk, she led me into the living room... (Raphael, 2003, p. *xix*)

As Susan Stocking wrote in a 1971 interview of Nin for *The Los Angeles Times*,

> In person, Anaïs Nin is the very essence of femininity. Her once dark hair, now blonde, is slightly parted in the middle, sweeping in gentle

half-moons from the center of her wide forehead, back over her ears and up into a modest roll atop her head.

> Her skin, though wrinkled and masked by makeup, seems ageless and opalescent as the insides of the seashell on her fireplace mantle. Her eyes, edged in heavy black mascara under Jean Harlow eyebrows, sparkle warmly in the midday sun. In shadow, they are invitingly cool pools of aquamarine. (Stocking, 1971/1994, p. 99)

And finally, in an interview for *The New York Post*, Fern Marja Eckman observed,

> There was Anaïs Nin...swathed in ankle-length black gown and white-lined swirl of shepherd's cape, her face serene and ageless, looking not unlike a medieval saint enshrined in a niche.....She smiled. It was an archaic Greek smile, a stone madonna's smile that curved her lips but left the rest of her features immobile. The green-dark eyes, sharply outlined in black and so large that they almost make her seem top-heavy, gazed out over that smile like a child peering over a fence. (Eckman, 1972/1994, p. 172)

A few comments on Nin's appearance included second-wave feminist interpretations of Nin's dress and philosophy as too essentialist and too feminine to be at home among the feminists of the 1960s and 1970s (Fitch, 1993; Jelinek, 1974; Tookey, 2003), as illustrated by the quotes from Fitch (1993), below:

> [Nin's] place in women's culture and literature has not been fully appreciated, in part because academic feminists are embarrassed by her delicate feminine personae. (Fitch, 1993, p. 8)

> [Nin's] appearance was exotic, her costume always impeccable. One friend described her as embodying a "touch of the geisha, a touch of the governess, and a touch of the Gish sisters." Just the kind of femininity to have raised Simone de Beauvoir's hackles. (Fitch, 1993, p. 5)

Despite the discourse on Nin's appearance, few scholars have focused on Nin's dress from the perspective of objective dress scholarship. Notable exceptions are an unpublished conference presentation by dress scholar Tove Hermanson (2010) and a short paper by Nin scholar and screenwriter Kim Krizan (Krizan, 2011). Krizan (2011) examined *Linotte: The Early Diary of Anaïs Nin, Volume 1: 1914-1920* (Nin, 1978), noting Nin's earliest journal writings on dress. For Krizan (2011), there was a connection between Nin's pain at the loss of her father (whom the family had left behind in Europe when her parents separated) and her growing love of dress. According to Krizan (2011), for the adolescent Nin, dress was "an obsession that seemed to grow right along with her writing" (Krizan, 2011, p. 111), even becoming "…an oasis of pleasure, a substitution for the love of an absent parent" (Krizan, 2011, p. 113). Although not a dress study, Nalbantian (1997) briefly examined some of Nin's writings on dress and masquerade, finding parallels in the diaries and her fiction and concluding, "Shedding and reclothing selves was to Nin as common as donning and removing clothes, for her aesthetic personality was in constant masquerade on a stage which was life" (Nalbantian, 1997, p. 12).

Cultural Context: Nin's Interwar Paris

The consensus among dress scholars is that the 1920s and 1930s were an important era from the perspective of everyday dress to *haute couture* (i.e., Hollander, 1982; Marcketti & Angstman, 2013). Feminist historians have especially highlighted the interwar years, the period between the end of World War I and start of the German occupation of France, 1919-1939, to have been of special interest to historians and feminist scholars (Doan, 1998; Weiss, 1995). The period in Nin's life examined in this study was significant not only for her, personally, but also because it is a rich era for scholarly inquiry. In the 1920s and 1930s, Paris was a unique nexus for experimental thought and design, particularly among women as designers and creators of fashion. Paris's history and role as a center for fashion consumption has long been noted by dress scholars (Rocamora, 2009; Steele, 1998).

> And what better place was there to be thirty and carefree than Paris, and especially Montparnasse? (Franklin, in Bald, 1987, p. *xxiii*)

Anaïs Nin was 28 and 29 years old while she penned the journals that were the primary sources for this study. She was married, did not have to work to earn a living, and was able to enjoy the cafés of Montparnasse. Like many Americans in Paris, she read Wambly Bald's weekly column in the Paris edition of the *Chicago Tribune*, "La Vie de Bohème (As Lived on the Left Bank)" about life in bohemian Montparnasse. Nin, however, did not socialize with the well-known literati of Paris (i.e., Gertrude Stein, James Joyce, Natalie Barney, or Janet Flanner, to name only a few). Nin and her family had lived in Montparnasse when they first moved to Paris years earlier, but did not move in those circles. The Guilers smoked Sultanes brand cigarettes (Entry dated May 7, 1932, Diary 34, p. 140), rather than "ordinary" Camel brand cigarettes (Diary 32, p. 234). With their family and friends, they went to the theatre and cinema. In Paris Nin saw Josephine Baker perform and watched Fritz Lang's "Metropolis," Luis Buñuel's "Un Chien Andalou," and von Sternberg's "Blue Angel" (Nin, 1985, p. 38, p. 338, p. 383).

By 1931, when this study's data collection began, Paris's Left Bank had undergone a change and was not the lively place it had been during the 1920s. Most of the Americans living in Montparnasse had returned to the United States, due to financial hard times. Henry Miller and his wife June Mansfield Miller had visited in the late 1920s; but not until 1930 did Henry Miller move to Paris to stay (Dearborn, 1991, p. 123). Nin visited Montparnasse, going to the Café du Dome and the restaurant Les Vikings, and cultivated the company of writers, but did not embrace bohemian life. As described above, in 1931 she lived in a small town outside of Paris, Louveciennes, with her family. She dressed relatively conventionally, following the fashions of the day. Whereas her journals of the late 1920s include mentions of her Russian dressmaker by name, Madame Vallia Melnikoff, by 1931 and 1932 she did not refer to her dressmaker by name and only sporadically (Nin, 1985; Diaries 32-36). In June 1931, she had evening dresses lengthened and a turquoise cape dyed black, in an effort to dress fashionably while cutting costs (Diary 31, p. 1). She was preparing to go abroad and the pre-travel shopping was intended to be her last big shopping for new clothing for the year. She had intended to hold off on making her first entry in a brand-new journal until she was travelling, but "bursting with a love" of dress, she found she just could not wait:

> June 5- A pair of black *glacé* gloves, a red picture hat, a little red jacket, a Robertson clan plaid skirt, the turquoise green cape dyed black, several evening dresses lengthened, new petticoats made out of artificial silk, much hunting after practical clothes and buying the unusual, a tremendous struggle to get myself into a tailor[ed] suit and

> final choice of dying my cape and asserting my semi-independence…Clothes. The worship of clothes. Pretext: preparations for the trip. Hugh says: get me a couple of ties and a sweater…I had not wanted to write here until we were in the train, but I was bursting with a love of costuming and the realization that it would all be for the last time because I must sober down in harmony with our new life. After all clothes are the trip. You begin to travel when you try on that red picture hat whose wings will flap so becomingly in the sea breeze. (Entry dated June 5, 1931, Diary 31, pp. 1-2)

The 1920s and 1930s saw increased use of artificial silk (called rayon until the 1950s), like that used for Nin's petticoats mentioned above (Tortora & Marcketti, 2015, p. 465). Hemlines, which had begun to lengthen in the late 1920s, came down even further in the early 1930s (Tortora & Marcketti, 2015, p. 473 & p. 481). Although bobbed hairstyles were popular in the 1920s, Nin did not wear her hair cut short, instead preferring to keep her hair long, sometimes cutting the sides short enough to allow her to mimic the bobbed look.

Design influences in Paris in the 1920s and 1930s included Art Deco and Surrealism (Gibson, 2003); the "mannish" style suit for women (Marcketti & Angstman, 2013), the fetishization of the art and culture of the African continent (Archer-Shaw, 2000), the "flapper" and "*garçonne*" phenomena, and Russian-inspired styles due to the influence of Russian emigrés in Paris (Vassiliev, 1998; Vaughan, 2006). The era also saw the continued existence of the Parisian couture and the celebrity designer; and women's continued roles as laborers and shop workers in the clothing and textiles trade (Clark, 1981; McMillan, 1981). Emerging technologies in dress design of the era included artificial fibers, zippers, and the bias cut (Tortora & Marcketti, 2015). Design piracy was a problem that plagued designers (Marcketti & Parsons, 2016; Pouillard, 2011). Also emerging in the 1920s and 1930s was the development and professionalization of cosmetic surgery in France. Practiced since the late eighteenth century, cosmetic surgery had become increasingly popular in France by Nin's era (Comisky, 2004; Davis, 1999; Martin, 2016).

The Use of Autobiography and Diaries as Source Material in Dress Studies

Texts, such as autobiography and diaries, have proved extremely valuable as primary sources for dress historians. There have been several studies on dress that have relied on personal writings such as diaries, memoirs, and autobiographies in recent years. Vaughan (2006) examined the journals and memoirs of Natacha Rambova and Rudolph Valentino in her study of Rambova's brief career as a *couturière* in 1928-1931. Autobiographical texts were also used by Sanders (2011), who examined references to appearance in published nineteenth-century African American female slave narratives. Adler (1980) examined the diary of an American woman who emigrated from Massachusetts to California for marriage and the author's writings on the preparation of her wedding dress, made before her arrival in California and held in the costume collection of San Francisco's M. H. de Young Memorial museum. Baumgarten (1996) examined published journals and letters from the eighteenth and early-nineteenth centuries in support of her paper on a maternity gown in the Colonial Williamsburg Foundation collection. Gordon (1987) examined a variety of written sources on the American Civil War and discussion of clothing and textile shortages; a number of those sources were published diaries and memoirs. Later, Gordon (1992) delved into nineteenth century American New England women's writings for information on dress using sources that ranged from diaries, etiquette manuals, popular fiction, and letters. In her study of the dress practices of students of Smith College, Van Cleave (2005) included diaries and letters among her primary sources. Dress scholar Rabine (2007) analyzed masquerade, sexuality, and subcultural identity in her analysis of the nineteenth-century travel memoir of Flora Tristan. Wrisley (2006) examined the published diary, unpublished autobiography, letters, and published magazine articles of nineteenth-century American dress-reform advocate Charlotte Perkins Gilman, whose autobiographical short story *The Yellow Wallpaper* (itself presented in the form of a secret diary kept against doctor's orders) is a classic in both American and feminist literature.

Chapter 3
Method

Overview

This chapter begins with a description of the data collection process and explains the researcher's process of determining which data to analyze for the purpose of this study. The rationale behind the decision to analyze data from six of Anaïs Nin's handwritten journals from 1931-1932 is explained in depth, and justification for this study's method is provided. The historical method is explained in detail, providing evidence of methodological soundness, reliability, and validity.

Method of Data Collection

This study employed Fitzpatrick's (2007) historical method and her "great person" approach (Fitzpatrick, 2007, p. 409):

> This approach focuses attention on individuals and their personal power within a social context. It is particularly useful when the objective is a biographical study…

This approach was selected as Nin herself, "liked to say it would take one hundred biographers to tell her story" (Fitch, 1993, p. 415). This study began with concurrent examination of the two authoritative biographies published on Nin (Bair, 1995; Fitch, 1993) and a close examination of the published versions of Nin's journals from the 1920s through the mid-1930s. The number of published journals has grown steadily since Nin's death in 1977, with the most recent volume published in 2017 (Nin, 2017). Selection of the published journals to examine was based on the chronological dates of the material contained within, i.e., the dates in which their text was penned, not published. Nin worked on preparation of her journals for publication until shortly before her death, and her second husband Rupert Pole, as her literary executor, carried on her work after her passing with the assistance of editors Gunther Stuhlmann and John Ferrone; translator Jean Sherman; Nin's brother, Joaquín Nin-Culmell; and in some instances, Nin's first husband, Hugh Guiler. It had been Nin's wish that publication of materials revealing her relationship with Henry Miller be delayed until after Guiler's death. Therefore, the journals from October 1931 onward were not published in their unexpurgated form until after Guiler's death in 1985. The published volumes examined in this study's preliminary analysis are listed below in chronological order, by the dates in which their content was originally written, with the date of publication in parentheses:

- *The Early Diary of Anaïs Nin, Volume 2: 1920-1923* (1982)
- *The Early Diary of Anaïs Nin, Volume 3: 1923-1927* (1983)
- *The Early Diary of Anaïs Nin, Volume 4: 1927-1931* (1985)
- *The Diary of Anaïs Nin: 1931-1934* (1966) *Henry and June, from A Journal of Love: The Unexpurgated Diary of Anaïs Nin, 1931-1932* (1986)
- *Incest, from a Journal of Love: The Unexpurgated Diary of Anaïs Nin, 1932-1934* (1992)
- *The Diary of Anaïs Nin, Volume 2: 1934-1939* (1967)
- *Fire, from a Journal of Love: The Unexpurgated Diary of Anaïs Nin, 1934-1937* (1995)

Examination of the published journals revealed an important point: The published journals were openly acknowledged to have been edited for publication, rather than verbatim reproductions of the original handwritten texts. For example, Rupert Pole's Editor's Note in *Linotte: The Early Diary of*

Anaïs Nin, Volume 1: 1914-1920 (Nin, 1978) stated: "Deletions have been made solely for the sake of producing a book of publishable length and sustained interest" (Nin, 1978, p. *ix*). Pole's Editor's Note in *The Early Diary of Anaïs Nin, Volume 2: 1920-1923* further clarified:

> The present volume was prepared from a typescript made by Anaïs in the late 1920s. As she typed, she left out passages she considered schoolgirlish or those in which she went on a little too long about nature. Most of these deletions have been respected, but in some instances significant material has been restored. The editorial approach is the same as for *Linotte*. *Cuts have been made in repetitious passages, extended quotations and routine entries of little interest to the reader.* (Nin, 1982, p. *vii*) [emphasis added]

However, what may be considered of little interest to the general reader may be of value to the dress historian. The concurrent examination of the Fitch (1993) and Bair (1995) biographies (both of which referenced Nin's handwritten journals) and the published diaries listed above revealed that, indeed, some details of Nin's thoughts and actions on dress, as recorded in her journals, had been excluded from the various published volumes of *The Diary of Anaïs Nin* (especially Nin, 1966 & 1986). To provide just one example, both Fitch (1993) and Bair (1995) noted that Nin had dyed her hair black sometime in late December 1931 or early January 1932 (Bair, 1995, p. 127, pp. 548-549,[1] & Fitch, 1993, p. 112). Mention of Nin having dyed her hair was not found in either *The Diary of Anaïs Nin: 1931-1934* (Nin, 1966) or *Henry and June* (Nin, 1986). Fitch (1993), when noting Nin's dyed hair color in February 1932 (Fitch, 1993, p. 112), cited both Nin's handwritten Diary 33 (Box 16, Folder 2, Anaïs Nin Papers, Collection 2066, UCLA) and *Henry and June* (Nin, 1986) (Fitch, 1993, p. 112 & endnote 58, p. 438). The early discovery of references to Nin's unpublished writings on dress practices noted by Fitch (1993) and Bair (1995) gave weight to this study's initial supposition that Nin's original journals contained unpublished writings on dress of interest to the dress scholar.

---

[1] According to Bair, the night Nin first met June Miller, Nin's hair had been dyed black, because "She had had it dyed especially for June because Henry had told her black was June's color..." (Bair, 1995, pp. 548-549).

Examination of *Henry and June* (Nin, 1986) found no mention of hair dye. However, investigation of the handwritten diaries revealed:

> This morning [January 16, 1932] I awoke to follow a crazy impulse and before I met June I had my gold-red-brown hair —so indefinite- dyed a deep blue-black. It was an effort to evade myself from my confining personality—the physical personality. My soft, pastel, indefinite coloring did not express my decisiveness and intellectual positivism. Now I am happy, although this constant effort I make not to be confined by a determinate personality seems ridiculous. (Nin, Diary 32, pp. 180-181)[2]

With the finding of this powerful quote, it became clear that the handwritten diaries contained significant information that would be valuable to understanding Nin's dress practices. This study focused its examination on Nin's handwritten diaries that were the source of the content in *Henry and June* (Nin, 1986). As explained earlier in this chapter, the rationale behind this decision was based on preliminary investigation into the published editions of Nin's diaries from the late 1920s and early 1930s (Nin, 1966, 1982, 1985, 1986, 1992, and 1995), plus a review of literature, including biographical works, on Nin and the body of literature. These works were largely editor-reviewed, but not peer-reviewed, Nin scholarship that sprang up since Nin's death in 1977. A concurrent reading of the two authoritative biographies of Nin (Bair 1995; Fitch, 1993) and Nin's published diaries revealed conflicting information. At first, this appeared to be plausible due to Deirdre Bair's (1995) status as the biographer "who had exclusive access to Nin's complete, original diary and the full cooperation of her surviving husband, family, and friends" (Bair, 1995, back cover matter, Penguin Books's American paperback edition; Herron & Bair, 2010). My decision to take Bair (1995) as the sole authoritative, and authorized, biography was based in part on the above and Bair's self-description as a biographer who spent "many months...poring over [Nin's] original diaries in the UCLA library," (Bair, 1995, p. *xvi*) and who wrote:

---

[2] In passages quoted from their respective journals, Nin's and Guiler's spelling and punctuation have been reproduced as written.

> As a biographer in the postmodern age, I still believe in trying to capture what others may consider anachronistic—the impugned, much disputed concept of objectivity. (Bair, 1995, p. *xvi*)

Examination of Nin (1986) continued, but taking Bair (1995) as an authority meant that any discrepancies between the facts of Nin's life as depicted in her published diaries and as related in Bair (1995) were tentatively dismissed as fabrications, embellishment, or simple alterations, on the part of Nin or her editors, based on Bair's (1995) portrayals of Nin's life, her diaries, and the diaries' publication process. Data on dress and appearance were collected from Nin (1986), Nin's handwritten diaries in UCLA, and the Anaïs Nin Collection in the Gleeson Library at USF (University of San Francisco, San Francisco, CA). Findings from primary sources, triangulated with Bair (1995), informed the decision to discount Bair's version of events and instead rely on Nin's words as presented in her journals (Nin, 1986; Diaries 32-36), for reasons which are explained below.

    I began collecting data from the Nin collections in UCLA and USF in the form of field notes and digital photographs which were reviewed and transcribed after the research visits. As described earlier in this chapter, a preliminary review of three volumes of Nin's posthumously published *Early Diary* series (Nin, 1982, 1983, & 1985) had revealed more mentions of everyday details of dress than were present in Nin 1966 and 1986, and the prefaces to Nin (1978) and Nin (1982), hinted at potential unpublished data to be found in the handwritten diaries in the Nin Collection at UCLA. Data collected at USF included the diary of Nin's husband, Hugh Guiler, and photocopies of Nin's typescript manuscripts for some of the diaries that became Nin (1985), which included handwritten corrections made by her brother, Joaquín Nin-Culmell. Also examined were several letters and faxes between Bair and Joaquín Nin-Culmell regarding the publication of the biography (Container 11, Folder 19), including descriptions of Bair's legal woes with Stuhlmann that resulted even before the biography was published. These letters and faxes revealed that both Nin's literary agent, Gunther Stuhlmann, and Nin's second husband, Rupert Pole, had severed ties with Bair as a result of the 1995 biography. As Stuhlmann wrote, in a letter to Bair, quoted by Bair in a letter to Nin-Culmell:

> One wonders, indeed, why the grasping, egotistical, monstrous slut that emerges from your pages should have had any

influence on anybody. You claim such compassion for Anaïs in your letter, but you are able to write about her birth story: 'It is a portrait of monstrous egotism and selfishness, horrifying in its callous indifference...' (Stuhlmann as cited, in a letter from Bair to Nin-Culmell, January 11, 1994, p. 1, Container 11, Folder 19, Anaïs Nin Collection, Gleeson Library, USF)

> Anaïs, we all agreed, deserves a sound, accurate, and understanding biography which established a relationship between the woman and the work, that went beyond sexual sensationalism, moralistic disapproval of her life, and offered some insight into her creative work and the ideas she tried to develop and pursue, the salvation she hoped to find in art.
> [T]hat book, I am afraid, has yet to be written. (p. 2, ibid)

This information, along with discrepancies observed between Bair (1995) and Fitch (1993), Nin (1986), and Diaries 32-36, supported the decision to disregard Bair's (1995) portrayal of Nin and investigate primary sources instead of limiting this study to an analysis of Nin (1986). Further explanation appears below.

The Author(s) and Editors of Henry and June

The posthumously published diaries (Nin, 1986) written in the time period this study addressed were not released until after the death of Nin's first husband, Hugh Guiler. Nin's second husband Rupert Pole, the heir to her literary works, worked with editor John Ferrone of Harcourt Brace Jovanovich to make *Henry and June* (Nin, 1986) a product that was quite distinct from *The Diary of Anaïs Nin, Volume 1, 1931-1934* (Pole & Ferrone, 2007; Nin, 1966 & 1986). A small amount of diary text that had been published in Nin (1966) was included in order to provide context, but for the most part *Henry and June* (Nin, 1986) contained only material relating to Nin's romantic relationships with Guiler, Henry and June Miller, and her cousin, Eduardo Sanchez, and her psycho-analytic sessions with her analyst, Dr. René Allendy (Pole & Ferrone, 2007; Nin, 1986, p. *ix*). Although uncredited in *Henry and June* (Nin, 1986), Ferrone took on the bulk of the editing process and the end result was a book intended to read like a romance novel (Pole & Ferrone, 2007). The process of editing, undertaken mostly by Ferrone but with much input from Pole, was at times tumultuous (Pole & Ferrone, 2007). Initially asked by Pole to create a book that would "focus on the love story" and be as successful as his prior editorial projects, Nin's best-selling erotica, *Delta of Venus* (1977) and *Little Birds* (1979), Ferrone shaped the diaries into a product designed to be markedly different from the several diary volumes already on the market (Pole & Ferrone, 2007, p. 18). Pole, however, wanted to remain as true as possible to Nin's original voice and diary entries, even arguing that the novel-like form that Ferrone sought to give *Henry and June* (Nin, 1986) was not true to Nin's style of writing:

> ...this is not a novel—it is Anaïs' diary, written by her in her unique style...We must honor her by preserving a few passages the way she wrote them. (Pole, as cited in Pole & Ferrone, 2007, p. 17)

John Ferrone, on the other hand, already regarded *Henry and June* (Nin, 1986) as embellished autobiography, rather than factual diary (Pole & Ferrone, 2007, p. 8). The work may be subtitled *"the unexpurgated diary,"* however, as Jarczok (2017) wrote, "differently expurgated," may be more apt (Jarczok, 2017, p. 152).

As an example of the differences between Nin's handwritten journals, Nin (1966) and Nin (1986), transcribed text from page 49 in Diary 33 (Figure 1) is presented below, compared to the text as it was later edited and published:

> I get letters from Henry every other day. I answer him immediately. I gave him my typewriter, and write by hand. I think of June day and night. I am full of incandescent energy: I write endless letters with the prospectuses [to sell her new book, Nin (1932)]. I see the ear specialist and get a reduction on his bill. I see Drake and measure his small stature (a small man is he who is always struggling desperately to <u>reduce</u> others. Drake reduces Henry – everybody he talks of.) I see the plumber about a gas leak. I order coal. I start a clay head of Hugh. I invent a costume. I take care of beautifying my body for hours. I perfume my black hair now. I brush and comb Ruby [her dog]. I light fires in the fireplaces. I see people. I dream of an extraordinary <u>extra</u> life I am going to lead on the side someday, which may even fill another and special diary. I never stop. I think too much—it hurts me. Last night, after reading Henry's novel, I couldn't sleep. (Box 16, Folder 2, Diary 33, pp. 49-50)

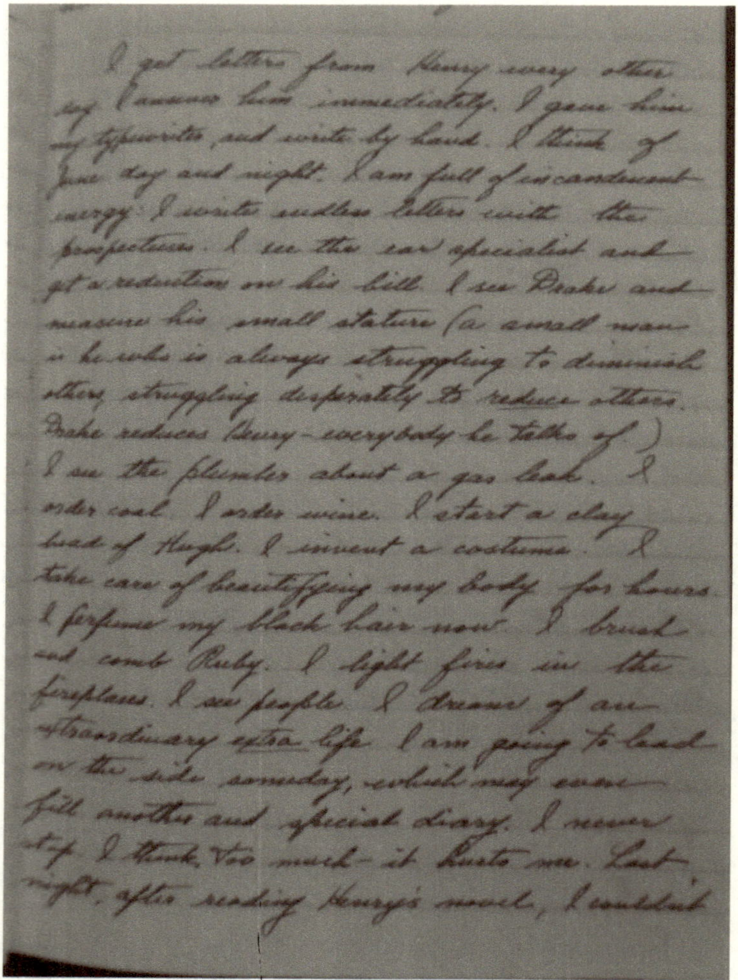

Figure 1. Photograph (detail) of page 49, Diary 33, Anaïs Nin Papers (Collection 2066). Library Special Collections, Charles E. Young Research Library, UCLA.

The above passage, appears in Nin (1966), coincidentally on page 49:

> I get letters from Henry every day. I answer him immediately. I gave him my typewriter and I write by hand. I think of June day and night. I am full of energy. I write endless letters.
> Last night after reading Henry's novel I could not sleep.

(Nin, 1966, p. 49)

And, as published in Nin (1986):

> I get letters from Henry every other day. I answer him immediately. I gave him my typewriter, and I write by hand. I think of him day and night.
> I dream of an extraordinary extra life I am going to lead someday, which may even fill another and special diary. Last night, after reading Henry's novel, I couldn't sleep. (Nin, 1986, p. 45)

The differences between the edited versions of the diary text and the original are significant and reveal information on dress that was previously unpublished: "I invent a costume. I take care of beautifying my body for hours. I perfume my black hair now" (Diary 33, p. 49). Jarczok (2017) also wrote that Ferrone's editing created an all new Nin persona who, compared to the Nin of *The Diary of Anaïs Nin, 1931-1934* (Nin, 1966) was "preoccupied with sexuality" (Jarczok, 2017, p. 152). That was this study's assessment as well. As Jarczok (2017) wrote:

> ...Ferrone dramatically changed Nin's self-presentation...Nin introduced herself in *Diary 1* [Nin, 1966] predominantly as a budding writer. The first pages of *Henry and June* [Nin, 1986] present a different Nin, a Nin...virtually absent from the first seven volumes [of published diaries]—the Nin preoccupied with sexuality. (Jarczok, 2017, p. 152)

Therefore, this study noted that the romantic storyline of *Henry and June* (Nin, 1986) and the new version of Nin contained within, were elements that set the book apart from Nin's previously published diaries and her handwritten diaries.

After reading Bair (1995), I was hesitant about taking anything written in the handwritten diaries or in Nin (1986) as fact, based on Bair's denigration of the value of Nin's diaries and Nin (1986) as worthwhile sources of information on a woman's subjective account of her lived, experience. As previously described, the editing process that created *Henry and June* (Nin, 1986) (according to Bair, 1995) made selection of Nin (1986) as an historical source a problematic choice. Bair quoted John Ferrone, editor of *Henry and June* (Nin, 1986) as describing Nin (1986) as having limited use as a reference:

> Consisting of excerpts from Anaïs Nin's typed transcripts of the original journals with interpolations of a few passages from volume one of the published diary, it is undependable as a reference. Therefore, it is of questionable use to scholars. (John Ferrone, as quoted in Bair, 1995, p. 518)

What Bair did not specify, however, was what kind of scholars would find Nin (1986) of limited value. Faucheux (2016), for example, found both Nin (1966) and (1986) as worthy of investigation in her proposed new reading model for texts of women's adultery and polyamory. Therefore, I began investigating and evaluating Nin (1986) as a potential sole data source for this study. Review of Nin scholarship and literature continued concurrent to data collection. Further review of the literature on Nin revealed that Bair's (1995) biography was not warmly welcomed by Nin scholars and fans and was denounced by those who knew Nin and her life and works intimately. This opened the door to this study's further exploration of Nin's works, in particular her diaries in UCLA and the documents at USF. As a dress historian I believed it necessary to investigate them as original source documents, as clearly Fitch (1993) and Bair (1995) had both had access to the diaries and both scholars noted details of dress that were not published in Nin (1966) or Nin (1986).

Despite the differences between the diaries in UCLA and the content of Nin (1986), I remained reluctant to rely exclusively on primary sources. Anaïs Nin's relationship with the truth has been explored by biographers and critics alike (e.g., Bair, 1995; Fitch, 1993; Jarczok, 2017; Tookey, 2003), and what made this study so challenging as an historical study was the way that both of the principal biographers of Nin immediately discredited Nin and her diaries at the opening of each of their book-length studies of her life:

> Why does a writer who kept a diary all her life need a biographer? *Because her diary itself is a work of fiction*, an act of self-invention. Untrue confessions....In short, her diary is not to be trusted. (Fitch, 1993, pp. 4-5) [emphasis in Fitch]

> The persons whose testimony I collected included those who had known her in varying degrees of friendship and intimacy, those who had merely read all or parts of her published diary (or "liary," as one called it), and those like the very young university students I

addressed in far-off Australia who told me all they knew about her was that "Nin had a lot of sex and lied a lot." (Bair, 1995, pp. *xv-xvi*)

Bair (1995) referred to data collected from those who had known Nin in life as "testimony" (Bair, 1995, twice on p. *xv*, & again on p. *xvii*) and referred again to Nin's diary as a "liary" two more times in her introduction (Bair, 1995, p. *xvii* & p. *xviii*), portraying herself as a biographer who conscientiously sought "testimony" from witnesses (and Australian college students) to separate the facts of Nin's life from her subjective experience contained in her, according to Bair, "liary." However, Nin (1986) continued to interest me as a potential period in Nin's life to investigate for this study. Complicating matters was Bair's continuing claim to have had exclusive access to Nin's diaries (Bair, 1995; Herron & Bair, 2010), which was not borne out by details presented in Fitch (1993), and has been refuted (Jarczok, 2017, p. 231).

Nin was often depicted by Bair (1995) as a sociopathic nymphomaniac whose diaries were filled with false information, raising concern about Nin and her diaries' worthiness as sources for serious study. For those reasons, I was both attracted and repelled as a scholar, ambivalent about investigating the handwritten diaries for unpublished evidence Bair had alluded to. Wondering whether the diaries were something I truly wanted to investigate, given their questionable portrayal in Bair (1995), I continued to collect and analyze data from Nin (1986) and the original diaries in order to determine whether to analyze Nin (1986) as a work of literature, or the diaries as historical primary source documents. Despite my ambivalence, it remained apparent, that Nin had led an intriguing life that was relatively unexamined by dress historians and that she had left written, contemporary accounts of her experience, now publicly accessible, which had, indeed, included detailed descriptions of her dress and body, and her attitudes and reflections on her appearance and potential connection to an "artificial personality" (Bair, 1995, p. 148) as revealed by Nin's dress.

As data collection and analysis continued, it became increasingly difficult to take Bair (1995) as an authoritative source for information on Nin's lived experience for the purposes of studying Nin's dress and appearance. Both Fitch (1993) and Bair (1995) were quick to establish Nin as an unreliable narrator of her own life, even within her own diaries. As this study progressed, and triangulation of the data in the archives and in Bair (1995) continued, it became apparent that there were several events in Nin's life in the early 1930s that appeared markedly different in Bair (1995) in comparison to how they appeared in Nin's published diaries and the handwritten diaries (for example, a striking difference between Nin's and Bair's descriptions of Nin's talks about her appearance with her psychoanalyst (e.g., Bair, 1995, pp. 147-148[3], as compared to Nin, 1986, pp. 144-145, & Diary 34, pp. 153-155), and Bair's strange denials of the intimacy of Nin and Eduardo Sanchez's relationship (cf., Bair, 1995, pp. 543[4] & 549[5]; Fitch, 1993, pp. 115-117; Nin, 1986, pp. 74 & 79, Diary 33, pp. 153-161, pp. 183-186, pp. 220-222, pp. 224-227, p. 231, & Diary 35, p. 52) and masturbation (cf., Bair, 1995, p. 549[6]; Fitch, 1993, p. 89, p. 96, p. 127, & p. 435; Nin, 1986, p. 130 & p. 180, Diary 34, p. 92, p. 97, pp. 283-284, & Diary 35, p. 16)). The discovery of these differences between Bair's (1995) and Nin's portrayals of events urged reconsideration of Bair's negation of the value of the handwritten diaries as sources for this study. Thus, this study made a transition from examination of Nin (1986) to a study that examined primary source documents.

---

[3] For example, Bair's versions of Nin's psychoanalytic sessions with Dr. Allendy:
> [Nin] turned the discussion to her body, pirouetting as she demonstrated how she was underweight and underdeveloped. Her breasts were too small, she said as she added calculatedly, "perhaps because I have masculine elements in me." He began to question why she felt this way, when she stood up and abruptly unbuttoned her blouse... (Bair, 1995, p.147)
> Each time [Allendy] questioned her too probingly, she turned the conversation to her body, particularly her breasts or her long legs. When she sat, she deliberately hitched her skirt above her knees. With her top button undone provocatively, she bent over and cupped his hand as he lit her cigarettes. (Bair, 1995, p. 148).

[4] According to Bair, "there is no written evidence or verifiable oral testimony to support the contention that [Nin] and [Sanchez] ever consummated their relationship" (Bair, 1995, p. 543).

[5] "There is no evidence in any of her unpublished writings...that they ever consummated their relationship sexually" (Bair, 1995, p. 549).

[6] In Bair's words:
> [Endnote] 34. I am the first of Nin's biographers to have had access to her entire UCLA archive as well as to relevant holdings by and about her in other libraries. I have interviewed most of the persons still alive in whom she might possibly confided details of her sexual activity, and I have been given access to privileged documents kept by several of her analysts. In all of this enormous mass of paper, there is no written evidence that [Nin] ever masturbated. She seems to have preferred to wait for an encounter with a man. (Bair, 1995, p. 549)

Primary Sources Utilized in the Study

Nin's handwritten journals dated 1914-1966 are in the Anaïs Nin Papers held by the Charles E. Young Research Library Department of Special Collections at the University of California, Los Angeles (Collection 2066, UCLA). The French scholar of diaries and autobiography, Philippe Lejeune (2009), examined handwritten diaries in great depth and his methods of analysis were of particular relevance to this study. In describing his study of nineteenth-century French girls' diaries, Lejeune emphasized the necessity of analyzing handwritten text for greater understanding of the subject, rather than use of typed transcripts:

> I can read printed text fast, but girls' diaries written in the nineteenth century do not allow this. It is impossible to skim the text or anticipate the next page. Large slanting handwriting, adorned capital letters, and the very light color of the fading ink prevent easy reading…This slowness, however, is an advantage. The time I need to read the diary is also time I can take to understand. It allows for more empathy. I withhold my judgement, and I learn to listen. (Lejeune, 2009, p. 132)

This perspective, preferring the experience of reading a handwritten journal to reading a typed transcript and the value of the handwritten word, informed the decision to examine the original, handwritten journals of Anaïs Nin. Three exploratory, day-long, research visits to the archives at UCLA were made in March and April of 2016 to examine the archive materials. A fourth, week-long, visit, funded by a Stella Blum Student Research Grant from the Costume Society of America, was made in November 2016. Data collection during those visits consisted of research notes and digital photography of pages of a sample of the journals from the 1920s and 1930s. The decision to examine journals from these dates was anchored around the opening date (late 1931) of both the first published volume of Nin's journals and the first unexpurgated volume (Nin, 1966 & 1986). The rationale behind this decision was based on Nin scholars' consensus that 1931 was a pivotal year for Nin's writing (as demonstrated in her choice to have her first published diaries [Nin, 1966] open with entries from late 1931), the timing of Nin's relationship with Henry and June Miller, whom she met in 1931, and the small mentions of dress in Fitch (1993) and Bair (1995) as noted above. Further, the importance of Nin (1966), which opened with entries from late 1931, cannot be over-emphasized, not just for its reflection of the personal life of the author and her development as a writer, but also for its place in women's literature. As Fitch acknowledged, "[Nin's] first diary [Nin, 1966] ...made literary history both for the genre of autobiography and for the women's movement" (Fitch, 1993, p. 4).

During the three, one-day visits made in March and April 2016, pages from two journals spanning 1922-1924 and all pages of 15 journals dating from 1927-1932, for a total of more than 4,400 hand-written pages, were digitally photographed. In the extended, four-day research visit in November 2016, the pages of 18 journals dating from 1921-1927 and 1932-1934 were photographed; two of the diaries examined in March and April 2016, dated 1923-1924 & 1927-1928 (Diaries 19 & 25, respectively) were re-photographed, for improved image clarity. More than 5,300 hand-written diary pages were photographed in November 2016. Two other one-day research visits, to view relevant documents in the Anaïs Nin Collection in the Gleeson Library at the University of San Francisco, were completed in February and May of 2017. Letters, postcards, photographs, and various other documents relating to Nin were examined, including a journal by Nin's husband, Hugh Guiler, with relevant data dated 1932.

The handwritten journals from which the book *Henry and June* (Nin, 1986) was composed, Diaries 32 through 36 (Nin, 1986, p. *ix*) comprise some six volumes (note that there are two diaries numbered 33: Diary 33 & Diary 33 *Bis*) and approximately 1,530 pages of handwritten text. The volume of diary entries from the period in Nin's life covered in Nin (1986), October 1931 through October 1932, is extensive, and the handwritten diaries were found to contain writings on dress that were omitted in both Nin (1966) and *Henry and June* (Nin, 1986). After each research visit, photographs of the diary pages were combined to create portable document format (pdf) files, for greater ease of reading and analysis. The pdfs of the diaries that were to become *Henry and June* (Nin, 1986), Diaries 32-36, were then printed double-sided, in black and white, and bound in plastic spiral and comb bindings. The same procedure was also followed for the diary of Hugh Guiler in the Anaïs Nin Collection at USF; the photographs of this journal were also combined into a pdf, printed in black and white, and inexpensively bound for greater ease of reading. The printed copies of the diaries were used as reading copies, and the pdfs were referred to when transcribing data relevant to this study. The rationale for this method of data collection analysis was again informed by Lejeune (2009):

> To get close to the truth of another person's diary, then, one must read a lot of it for a long time. A diary is a dark room that you enter from a brightly lit exterior. It is so dark in there that you can't see a thing, but if you stay there for half an hour, you begin to see outlines, silhouettes begin to emerge from the shadows, you begin to make things out. (Lejeune, 2009, p. 181)

While in-person reading of the manuscript diaries, cover-to-cover, would most closely match Lejeune's (2009) philosophy, digital photography of the diaries and printing of the pdfs of the diaries, for later reading, was more time and cost effective, given the time and expense required to travel to the archives in Los Angeles. This digital photography also reduced potential wear and tear from overhandling of the physical manuscripts themselves, out of concern for their delicate nature and historical significance. Digital and printed images of the diaries permitted such necessities as repeated reading, making comparisons across various manuscript entries in multiple volumes, and even zooming in for closer inspection of Nin's relatively small handwriting. All of these benefits enabled the researcher to, as Lejeune recommended, "read a lot of [the diaries] for a long time" to an extent not possible in the actual archives (Lejeune, 2009, p. 181).

The diaries (both Nin's and Guiler's) were then read from cover to cover and all text relevant to dress, appearance, and the body was transcribed into Word documents for analysis. The same data was transcribed from Nin (1986), again selected for text on dress, appearance, and the body. Comparison of the handwritten diaries' data and *Henry and June* (Nin, 1986) revealed that the data from the primary sources were richer and revealed more information on dress, appearance, and the body.

Diary 33 and Diary 33 Bis

This study examined in depth Nin's journals that were the source material for Nin (1986): Diary 32, 33, 33 *Bis*, 34, 35, and 36. Regarding Diary 33 *Bis*, the UCLA Finding Aid for the Anaïs Nin Papers, Collection 2066 (2004[7]) described Diary 33 as being filed in Box 16, in Folder 2 (which it was on all visits in 2016), and noted:

---

[7] http://oac.cdlib.org/findaid/ark:/13030/kt3489p4x9

> There is a second diary 33, lacking a cover, beginning February 16, "Today I gave up the other journal...," pages unnumbered. (Finding Aid for the Anaïs Nin Papers, 2004, p. 11)

The book is missing a spine and only five signatures remain. It is similar to Nin's other journals from the same time period, and in my opinion would probably originally have been thicker and had more pages. In Nin's hand on the title page of this Diary 33 *Bis*, the diary is numbered "33^". Diary 33, the larger Diary 33, intact and with a dark red leather cover, which Nin refers to as "the red journal" in Diary 34 (Diary 34, p. 75, p. 116, p. 140, & p. 172).

The second Diary 33 appears to have caused some confusion for Nin scholars and biographers, in that Nin described in Diary 44 her creation of a diary with entries dated as being from the same period as the entries in Diary 33 (which was penned February-April, 1932). In the fall of 1933, Nin described in Diary 44 how she prepared a journal for the eyes of her husband, one that described her blossoming relationship with Henry Miller in early 1932 as merely a platonic friendship (Nin, 1992, p. 271 & Diary 44, p. 112; Nin & Miller, 1987, p. 212). Nin scholar Simon Dubois Boucheraud (2012) referred to the second Diary 33 in UCLA as "Journal 33 *bis*" (Boucheraud, 2012, p. 22). Bair (1995), who referred to them as the red diary and the green diary, appeared to have transposed the two, and attributed many of the details found in the Diary 33 *Bis* to Diary 33. Perhaps she had access to a third Diary 33, with a green cover, not present in the collection at UCLA.

In my own examination, Diary 33 *Bis* is missing a cover, as the Finding Aid describes, and retains its front green endpaper: this may be why Bair called it the "green diary," or perhaps it once had a red cover, which would account for her description of its content as having been from a red diary. Bair, who described Nin as an unreliable narrator of her own life and "liary," dated the day of Nin's husband's discovery of Diary 33 as having taken place in the March or April of 1932 (Bair, 1995, p. 132). In my research, I found that Nin described this discovery of Hugh's as taking place in the fall of 1933, in a diary entry dated October 1, 1933, more than a year later (Nin, 1992, pp. 268-269, & Diary 44, pp. 95-100).

Nin scholar Simon Dubois Boucheraud (2012) wrote of how he dated the earlier entries in Diary 33 *Bis* to the spring of 1932, in agreement with Fitch (1993) and Bair (1995) to some degree, and Boucheraud dated later entries to October 1933. Given the changes I observed in Nin's handwriting across the various entries, this conclusion is reasonable. Boucheraud's supposition was that when Nin made mention of considering starting a fictitious diary to Hugh in the spring of 1932, she had actually started writing one, but then abandoned it until Hugh read the Diary 33 in October 1933, at which point she resumed making entries in Diary 33 *Bis*. The entries in Diary 33 *Bis* are dated February 1932 through May *1933*, and those that are dated 1933 appear to have been so dated in error, as the entries in this diary reproduced the content of some entries in Diaries 33 and 34 (diaries written in February through May 1932), minus details of Nin's affairs with Henry Miller and Eduardo Sanchez.

Method of Data Analysis

To answer the research question, this study began with a very close reading of primary and secondary sources, with the use of open coding, looking for emerging themes, reading and re-reading the texts, and constantly evaluating the researcher's conclusions, while keeping in mind the spirit of the times in which Nin lived. All data on dress, appearance, and the body in Nin (1986), Nin's Diaries 32-36, Hugh Guiler's journal, and secondary sources (Dick, 1967; Bald, 1987) were transcribed into Word documents for coding and analysis. During the process of data collection and analysis, the researcher held in mind this study's central research question, "What was Anaïs Nin's dress and appearance, as described in her handwritten journals dating from 1931-1932?" As the process of narrowing down the data sample on which to focus proceeded, the decision was made to limit this study's data sample to six of the handwritten diaries and other sources as described above. As a qualitative study using the historical research method (Fitzpatrick, 2007), data collection and analysis took place simultaneously and the researcher used the constant comparative process of data analysis (Glaser & Strauss, 1967; Merriam, 2009; Merriam & Tisdell, 2016). To return to Lejeune (2009), diaries lend themselves particularly to the method of open coding, as the very practice of keeping a diary means a diarist has the tendency to be

> ...methodical, repetitive, and obsessive...In the tapestry of your life, you follow very specific threads, and only a small number of them. Just four letters, *a*, *b*, *c*, and *d*, are usually enough to flag the contents of a single diary. (Lejeune, 2009, pp. 179-80)

An initial coding guide for Nin (1986) was developed concurrent with analysis, which lent support to the necessity of a study of Nin's dress practices as recorded in her personal writings. Preliminary coding revealed a large volume of data on dress practices, justifying this study and the use of the diaries as source material. Themes or categories of data on Nin's dress practices that emerged included the following:

1. Nin's Dress and Appearance Practices: 1931-1932
    a. Nin's Dress for Day
    b. The Millers Come to Dinner: June Miller's Appearance as Related to Nin's
    c. Nin's and June Miller's Shoes
    d. Cosmetics (Lip Rouge, Powder, and Nail Polish):
        i. Nin's make-up
        ii. nail polish
        iii. June Miller's make-up
    e. Perfume
        i. The scent of the diaries
    f. Hairstyling
    g. Jewelry
    h. Undergarments
    i. Evening dresses
    j. Outerwear
    k. Hats and turbans
    l. Other accessories
    m. Sleepwear and loungewear
    n. Cosmetic surgery
    o. Spanish dance costume.
2. Body image.
    a. The effects of Henry Miller's appraisal of Nin's appearance.
3. Nin's abiding love of luxury within a bourgeois-bohemian tension.

Reliability and Validity

Throughout the study, an audit trail, in the form of descriptive notes of each of the diaries examined, field notes, reflective memos, and a research journal, was maintained to document each step in the research process. The data sample, besides being based on Nin (1986), was also selected for its representativeness, as a one-year sample of data from Nin's many years of diary keeping. As the coding guide was created, it was shared with the major professor for feedback and to limit any possible subjective bias of just one individual examining the work. Iterations from this sharing and in-depth examination of the diaries resulted in the final coding guide which was then applied to the primary and secondary sources described above. The published diaries (Nin, 1986) were read concurrently with the handwritten diaries (Diary 32-36) and the Bair (1995) biography. Discrepancies between the handwritten diaries, the published diaries, and Bair (1995) were noted, as a way to cross-check and triangulate sources. As described above, data in Bair (1995) had to be largely dismissed when it became clear that it was undependable as a reference. Meticulous records of every instance of dress or clothing as written about in the diaries have been kept. To further increase reliability, I have used Nin's own words to offer thick, rich descriptions.

Theoretical Framework

As the data were collected, theoretical frameworks were searched for possible explanation for the diaries. Freud (1933/1961), Rivière (1929), and Lacan (1985) were examples of psychoanalytic theory that were contemporary to Anaïs Nin's life and experience in the 1930s and which have been adopted (or critiqued) by feminist theory, including Tseëlon (1997). The work of Goffman (1959) is a foundational text in sociology and for those who study the social psychology of dress. Work on fashion and the body from Foucault (1977/1995) was also read to help ground the researcher in the ideas of the body as Nin's diaries were analyzed. Butler's (1997 & 2007) work on gender performativity connected to the psychoanalytic theorists, the philosophers, and Goffman (1959). Tseëlon's (1997) theoretical framework was closely examined, as it seemed to initially provide the most relevant framework for examining Nin's text. However, upon closer review, only one of Tseëlon's (1997) five paradoxes discussed below seemed relevant to Nin and her writing.

Social psychologist and dress scholar Efrat Tseëlon (1997) developed a conceptual framework presented in the book *The Masque of Femininity: The Presentation of Woman in Everyday Life* (1997). In *Masque*, Tseëlon drew on postmodernism, social-psychology, psychoanalytical theory, and feminist perspectives and epistemologies as she explored five paradoxes in the dress of Western women. Calling her method "creative critical analysis," Tseëlon created what she described as a "dialogue between analytic knowledge and creative readings of social phenomena" (Tseëlon, 1997, p. 2). Tseëlon's (1997) creative critical analysis examined a variety of postmodern and historical texts, and incorporated theory from sociology, psychology/psychoanalysis, literature, religion, feminist studies, and semiotics (Tseëlon, 1997, p. 2). The result was an epistemological framework that was particularly relevant to Nin and Nin's writings on appearance, given Nin's subjective position in the early twentieth-century and her interest in dress and in psychoanalysis in the 1930s. In highlighting cultural and historical discourse on the deception inherent in femininity, for example, Tseëlon (1997) recalled the psychoanalytic perspective that regarded femininity as masquerade (Freud, 1933/1961; Rivière, 1929; Tseëlon, 1997, p. 34). Tseëlon's (1997) five paradoxes concerning the dress of Western women are:

1. The modesty paradox—the woman is constructed as seduction—to be forever punished for it.

2. The duplicity paradox—the woman is constructed as artifice, and marginalized for lacking essence and authenticity.

3. The visibility paradox—the woman is constructed as a spectacle while being culturally invisible.

4. The beauty paradox—the woman embodies ugliness while signifying beauty.

5. The death paradox—the woman signifies death as well as the defense against it. (pp. 5-6)

This study's data were coded for each of Tseëlon's (1997) Five Paradoxes. Paradox 3 was found to be the most applicable to the data. This finding is discussed in Chapter 5.

Chapter 4
Results

Overview

This study's purpose was to discover Anaïs Nin's dress, appearance, and dress practices as expressed in her journals upon which *Henry and June* (Nin, 1986) was based. The researcher examined Nin (1986) and the handwritten journals which were the source of the text within Nin (1986). This chapter presents the key findings obtained from close examination of Nin's handwritten journals, Journals 33 through 36 (Nin Papers, Collection 2066, UCLA), as well as findings from the handwritten journal of Nin's husband, Hugh Guiler, housed in the Gleeson Library (Anaïs Nin Collection, USF), Kenneth C. Dick's (1967) biography of Henry Miller, for which June Miller was interviewed extensively; Wambly Bald's January 12, 1932 newspaper article on June Miller, pasted into Nin's Diary 32 (Bald, 1987, pp. 87-89); plus data on June Miller from two other articles by Bald (Bald, 1987, p. 91 [January 19, 1932] & p. 142 [July 25, 1933]).

Findings on Nin's dress in 1931-1932 include an overview of Nin's appearance, apparel (day dresses, stockings, shoes, cosmetics, perfume, hairstyling, jewelry, undergarments, evening dresses, outerwear, hats and turbans, accessories, sleepwear and loungewear) cosmetic surgery, Spanish dance costume, body image, the effects of Henry Miller's appraisal of her appearance, and Nin's abiding love of luxury. The similarities between Nin's and June Miller's will also be explored as they reveal context relevant to understanding Nin's dress and appearance. Because it would be impossible to discuss Nin's dress without discussing June Miller's influence, and by extension, June's dress practices, the two women's dress will be discussed as it appeared in the diaries and secondary sources, in chronological sequence.

Overview of Nin's Dress and Appearance Practices: 1931-1932

Anaïs Nin lived the simultaneously busy and yet leisurely life of an upper-middle class married, European-American woman in 1931-1932. Her husband was employed as a banker and supported a household that included Nin, her mother, her brother, and two Spanish maids. The family's home in Louveciennes, France, was a short train ride outside of Paris, and the Guilers and Nin's mother and brother maintained separate living quarters in their shared house. The Guilers and Nin's family often entertained visiting family and friends, and the Guilers often entertained bank contacts and clients of Hugh's. In addition, Nin's brother, Joaquín Nin-Culmell, was a music student who attended school in Paris and the family often attended musical evenings in the city.

Nin's everyday life was primarily filled with writing, caring for the home, shopping, posing for the painter Natasha Troubetskoia, sessions with her psychoanalyst, lunch, tea, and dinner in Paris, entertaining at home, attending films, plays, and musical events in Paris, gardening and walks in the nearby forest on the weekends, and annual summer vacations to Switzerland, Spain, and the south of France. Nin went to cafés in bohemian Montparnasse, the restaurant Les Vikings and the Café du Dôme, with her cousin, Eduardo Sanchez, dilettante and erstwhile painter, and Henry and June Miller. By the spring of 1932, Nin spent more time in Clichy, at and around the apartment Henry Miller shared with Alfred "Fred" Perlès, on the Avenue Anatole France (Cross, 1991, p. 28). Nin described going to her dressmaker, the Printemps department store in Paris, and her hairdresser, as part of her busy "society life" (Diary 34, p. 310). She also "renovated" and mended clothing and altered her hats (Diary 33, p. 24).

Mentions of acquiring items of dress that appeared in the diaries were often part of longer lists of everyday activities:

> I go to teas, to the dressmaker, the hairdresser, I see [Dr.] Allendy, Eduardo, Henry... (Entry dated May 22, 1932, Diary 34, p. 218)

> May 22. Have no time to write everything. Had to work on Allendy's article. I go to teas, the dresmaker [sic], the hairdresser. (Entry dated May 22, 1932, Diary 33 *Bis*, p. 111[8])

> ...the day's monotony...The day's white threaded continuity—wheel turning_ _ sweet but insipid habits. Breakfast. The cuff links on Hugh's shirt. The goodbye kiss. Orders to Emilia. Work. Dressing. The train. Society life... (Diary 34, p. 310)

> Efforts to live externally. Went to the hairdresser, shopping, to see Natasha, the dressmaker. (Entry dated June 12, 1932, Diary 35, p. 20)

In addition to her mentions of dress for everyday and special occasions, Nin also recorded her dreams in her diaries. These dream descriptions often included details of dress that had special significance to Nin in the context of interpreting the meanings of her dreams. In one dream in particular, Nin shopped for a second-hand dress and was saddened to be unable to afford to purchase it when she learned the price:

> I was in a market. I wanted to buy a second hand purple dress. The woman who sold it didn't know the price. She gave me a letter and asked me to help her look it up. The letter was a book, like a catalogue of wall papers. I turned the pages, and saw beautiful colors, arranged in tone scales _ I came to the purples. The purple dress was 125 frs. I couldn't afford it. I turned away disconsolately. (Diary 35, p. 139)

At the top of a page, early in one of her diaries, Nin began a list for herself, by writing across the top of the page: "Plan for Absolute Originality" (Diary 36, p. 6). She appears to have reconsidered whether such a plan was really feasible in life, for she then wrote:

---

[8] Although the pages of Diary 33 *Bis* were unnumbered by Nin, I refer to them by number, page 1 being the first page of text following the title page, on which the first entry, dated February 16 [1932], begins.

> I cannot plan for it. It comes unexpectedly, when I am choosing writing papers, a pair of shoes, an ash tray, a perfume, a Christmas card, a bottle of ink, a material for a dress. (Diary 36, p. 6)

Above Nin expressed that her "originality" in life was often tied to her decisions made when shopping for the tools of her profession (ink and writing papers), a decorative object for the home (the ash tray), and, second to the writing papers, shoes, perfume, and fabric for a dress. She also used shopping as a means for distraction, something she called "basking in trivialities" that brought what she called a "puerile joy," while at the same time aware of the value of those activities to affect her mood, entertain herself, and distract her from boredom:

> ...I am running away from myself until tomorrow when I see Allendy and Henry! Play my usual trick of going shopping, going on errands to luxurious places, basking in trivialities all related to dressing, embellishment etc. What symbolism in the quest for perfume, powder—a new handbag, new gloves—the puerile joy of the woman! (Entry dated September 21, 1932, Diary 36, p.108)

One of the more common observations June Miller, and others made about Nin's appearance and bearing was that she was soft spoken, graceful of movement, and walked with a "glide":

> Anais greeted them [the Millers] warmly in her soft tiny voice. (Dick, 1967, p. 199)

> Her hands were delicate and graceful, her poise and bearing perfect, and she spoke in almost hushed tones. (June Miller, in Dick, 1967, p. 199)

> [June Miller:] You are the most graceful woman I have ever seen. You glide when you walk... (Diary 32, p. 135)

> I walk about in feline, seductive movements... (Diary 34, p. 208)

Sometimes, however, this gentle image that she knew others had of her frustrated Nin:

> Curse my image, the image of me which faces me everyday [*sic*] with the same quivering over-fineness, the pride, the decadent aristocracy, the utter sense of beauty- - curse my eyes which seem deep and sad and truthful. Curse my hands which are delicate..[two periods] my walk which is a glide, my voice which is a whisper..[two periods] (Entry dated February 16, 1932, Diary 33, p. 54)

As the quotes on Nin's appearance in the 1960s and 1970s in Chapter Two demonstrated, descriptions of Nin's appearance tended to include mention of her eyes, and no one seemed able to agree on what color Nin's eyes were:

> "bright brown" (Raphael, 2002, p. *xix*)
> "invitingly cool pools of aquamarine" (Stocking, 1971/1994, p. 99)
>
> "green-dark" (Eckman, 1972/1994, p. 172)

Nin described June Miller, too, as having found Nin's eye color intriguing:

> She says, staring intently: ["]I thought your eyes were blue. They are strange and beautiful—grey and gold—with those black long lashes." (Diary 32, p. 135)

Eduardo Sanchez called them "green and demoniac [*sic*]" (Diary 36, p. 77).

Nin's Dress for Day

Nin wrote of how she wore a number of different dresses in her diaries, and in early 1932 those that received mention were described in the context of her relationship with June Miller: dresses she wore when with June or when thinking of June. Years later, June Miller described what Nin was wearing the evening the two women met, when Henry and June Miller went to the Guilers' home for dinner on December 29, 1931[9]:

> She was wearing a magnificent velvet orange gown with tiers of lace ruffles and lace cuffs. Her nails were painted crimson red, quite startling in those days when most women used neutral color polish or simply powder-buffed their nails. Her hair, blond with a slight tint of red, was superbly styled. (Dick, 1967, p. 199)

In Nin's diary, the dress Nin wore that evening was described as being "rose" in color, rather than orange. June Miller admired it so much apparently, that she asked Nin to gift her with it:

> She says she wants to keep the rose dress I wore the first night she saw me. (Diary 32, p. 147)

June Miller went on to describe the Guilers' home, which Nin had decorated, and how Nin comported herself:

> "In fact," recalls June, "Anais had elegant taste not only in clothes but in the selection of furniture and color schemes – soft apple-green walls complimented [*sic*] by silk drapes of russet, the rugs, the lighting – all were harmonious." (Dick, 1967, p. 199)

The color rose "old rose" seems to have either been a common choice for Nin for her day dresses, or a favorite dress. When June Miller visited Nin at home on January 11, 1932, Nin wore a dress described as being "old rose color" with a black velvet jacket:

> What a lovely way you have of dressing. This dress—its old rose color, its old fashioned fulness [*sic*] at the bottom – the little black velvet jacket, the lace color [*sic*, color, not collar], the lacing over the breasts – how perfect – absolutely perfect. I like the way you <u>cover</u>

---

[9] The date of Nin's and June Miller's first meeting was recorded by Nin as December 29, 1931 (Diary 32, "Journal of Facts," n. pag.).

yourself, too, there is very little nudity—just your neck, really...
(Diary 32, p. 157)

In the passage above, Nin wrote the words "lace color," in Nin (1966, p. 30) and Nin (1986, p. 22) this was corrected to read "lace collar." Nin later wrote that she wore an old rose dress with a black bodice which laced closed and had a black lace collar (Diary 32, p. 199). Whether this was the dress Nin wore on the evening of December 29, 1931, which June Miller had asked for or not is unclear, but it does seem to match the description of the dress worn by Nin on the afternoon of January 11, 1932, attributed to June Miller, above. Nin apparently did not intend to gift this particular dress, for she wore it to tea at Tierem Boyard, a Russian tea room (Diary 32, p. 199 & "Journal of Facts," n. pag.; Bonney & Bonney, 1929, p. 245), with June Miller on June's last day in Paris before she returned to New York, and wore it especially for June:

> I had dressed ritually for her, in the very costume which created a void between me and other people – a costume which was a symbol of my individualism and which she alone would understand. Black turban, old rose dress with black laced bodice, and black lace collar, old rose coat with Medici collar. I had created a sensation as I walked, and I was lonelier than ever, because the sensation was partly hostile, mocking, flattering, but not comprehensive. (Diary 32, p. 199)

The Millers Come to Dinner: June Miller's Appearance as Related to Nin's

June Miller's everyday dress, by contrast, was theatrical and bohemian. The Guilers first met June Miller when they invited the Millers to their home for dinner on December 29, 1931 (Diary 32, "Journal of Facts," n. pag.). Kenneth C. Dick's (1967) biography of Henry Miller and Wambly Bald's (1932/1987) article on June Miller that appeared in the Paris edition of the *Chicago Tribune* provided some information on June Miller's appearance and dress which will be discussed before data from Nin's diaries. According to Dick (1967), June and the Millers' friend Richard Osborn waited in the Café du Dôme in Montparnasse while Henry went for his first meeting with Nin, arranged by Osborn, whereas Nin's diary recorded her first meeting with Henry Miller as lunch with Osborn at her home (Diary 32, pp. 76-77 & entry for December 5, 1931, "Journal of Facts,":: "Dec. 5 – Osborn & Henry Miller for lunch," Diary 32, n. pag.).

> When Henry finally showed up around nine o'clock that night, June asked:
> "Well, how did it go?"
> Henry who ordinarily would have been babbling away without being asked was slow to answer and when he did it was:
> "Oh, so-so."
> "I never knew Henry to be so tongue-tied," said June, "and when I saw that odd expression on his face I said to myself – 'oh, oh, he's hooked.[']"
> "What do you mean, 'so-so'. Is it good or bad?" she persisted.
> "It may take some time," said Henry.
> Then a long silence before June said:
> "Oh well, tell us what Anais is like."
> "Anais? A bird."
> "What kind of a bird."
> "I don't remember." (Dick, 1967, p. 198)

Recalling their first dinner together, June Miller described her dress that evening to Dick (1967, p. 199). Henry Miller had been unable to describe Nin's appearance to his wife in advance, having been too "tongue-tied," (Dick, 1967, p. 199), but having heard that the Guilers' home was "elegant," and suspecting that Henry Miller had found Nin attractive, June Miller dressed accordingly, intending not to be shown up and to "shock":

> One evening the Millers were invited to the Guilers['] for dinner at Louveciennes. June, having rather surmised that it would be done on an elegant scale and that Anais, if she were taken in by Henry, would be dressed to the teeth, and again, June not wishing to come out second best in a fashion contest donned a red velvet dress with a hole in the elbow of one of the sleeves, the usual heavy cape, and topped off her shoulder length hair, now blond, with a large soiled slouch hat.
> "I wanted to look like a tramp. I wanted to shock, to bring Henry back to reality…" (Dick, 1967, p. 199)

Echoing Dick (1967), Nin wrote that June Miller wore a cape the second night the Guilers had the Millers to dinner, but it was not "the usual heavy cape" that Dick had described above ("Jan 2 - rest. Dinner f. Miller & June. Grand Guignol," Diary 32, "Journal of Facts," n. pag. & p. 137). After dinner, the two couples went to the theatre in Paris, the Grand Guignol, and according to Nin, June Miller's cape was velvet and not warm enough for the winter evening: "She shivers with cold under her light velvet cape" (Diary 32, pp. 136-137).

In addition to Nin's diaries, other detailed contemporary accounts of June Miller's appearance come from the "La Vie de Bohème (As Lived on the Left Bank)" weekly column in the European edition of the *Chicago Tribune* by Wambly Bald (1987). As Nin herself inserted a copy of the column dated Tuesday, January 12, 1932 (Bald (1987, pp. 87-89) in Diary 32, the text below is transcribed from the clipping found in the diary:

> She wears the mask of death and her ghastly beauty makes them stare. She crosses the street and walks into the [Café] Select. An audience is born. Montparnasse is just a stage for June Mansfield.
>
> There is something shadowy, drugged, about her speech; and when she talks to you, the ground slips from under your feet. She creates a certain atmosphere of unreality and you feel that her words lift you in a cloud of incense and leave you without a ladder......
>
> Her hair is generally pinned high in back, or she lets it fly in the wind. Last year her hair was purple, the year before it was mauve, next year it will be platinum. Now it is dyed a gold-kissed rust, almost red. Her eyes are wide apart and very deep, like a pair of tawny pits. And I admired her anaconda throat.
>
> "People hate me because I destroy them," June said. "I awaken their slumbering vices. Destruction may be very beautiful." She added that she considered herself a female Stavrogin [from Dostevsky's *Demons*]. The mask grinned at me, and I felt very shy. (Bald, January 12, 1932)
>
> ...she runs down to the [Café du] Dôme, orders a chartreuse, and Montparnasse rubs its eyes. The curtain goes up. June loves her audiences.
>
> They stare at her. They wonder about her cat's eye earrings [of] which she never wears more than one at a time....Her hats!

> There is one, à la Watteau, backed with a tuft of flowers, which she sports with a velvet cape and shantung dress. There is something inconsistent about a velvet cape, shantung dress and no stockings. (Bald, January 12, 1932)

In her description of June Miller's appearance the night they met, Nin wrote that June Miller's dress was black velvet, not red (Diary 32, pp. 122-129). She also described June Miller's face as having been very pale that night, and even "mask-like," on other occasions:

> Dec. 30 A startlingly white face—burning eyes. June Mansfield, Miller's wife…[ellipse in AN's text]As she came towards me from the darkness of my garden, into the light of the door I saw for the first time the most beautiful woman on earth. (Entry dated December 30, 1931, describing seeing June Miller for the first time on December 29, 1931, Diary 32, p. 122)

> A startlingly white face retreating into the darkness of the garden. (Diary 32, p. 126)

> Her blond hair, pallid face, demoniac arched, peaked eyebrows, a side cruel smile with a disarming dimple. (Entry dated January 4, 1932, describing having seen the Millers on January 2, 1932, Diary 32, p. 130)

> … she sits resplendent, with a mask-like face. (Diary 32, p. 133)

Other than writing that June Miller had wanted her "rose dress" that she had worn the first night the Millers came to dinner, Nin did not describe what she wore the evening she and June first met. Henry Miller had returned from having lunch with the Guilers having described Nin as looking like a bird (Dick, 1967, 198).

Bair (1995) wrote that Nin had dyed her hair black as a means of impressing June Miller ("had had it dyed especially for June because Henry told her black was June's color" (Bair, 1995, pp. 548-549), before meeting her for the first time. According to Bald (1987), June Miller in Dick (1967), and Nin in Diary 32 (p. 130), however, Miller's hair was some shade of blonde in December 1931 and January 1932. Fred Perlès described June Miller's hair as being dyed black in the autumn of 1932, as it had been the first time he had met her, a few years prior. As it was described as having gone through several color changes in Bald (1987), perhaps she had changed it in the interim and then re-dyed it black by the autumn of 1932:

> "No more quiet days in Clichy," wrote Perlès. "Two days after she moved in I felt as if I were in an insane asylum. She talked incessantly…[ellipse in Dick's text] There was an air of permanent intoxication about her, as though she were taking drugs…[ellipse in Dick's text] her face was a trifle paler and her jet-black hair had grown a little longer and a little blacker still. The same theatrical make-up, the same actress air; she still wore the long flowing cape she had the first time I met her with Jean Kronski at the Dôme." (Perlès, as cited in Dick, 1967, p. 201)

Whether Henry Miller had told Nin that his wife had dyed black hair before the two women were introduced was not mentioned in Diaries 32-36. After examining Diary 32, as a whole and its "Journal of Facts" at the end, I also did not find evidence that Nin had dyed her hair before meeting June Miller for the first time in December 1931. Nin did appear, however, to have had her hair newly dyed black at 9:00 am on January 16, 1932, before meeting June briefly at midday (Diary 32, "Journal of Facts," n. pag.), as she wrote in her journal:

> This morning I awoke to follow a [then, page 181:] crazy impulse and before I met June I had my gold-red-brown hair —so indefinite- dyed a deep blue-black. It was an effort to evade myself from my confining personality—the physical personality. My soft, pastel, indefinite coloring did not express my decisiveness and intellectual positivism. (Diary 32, pp. 180-181)

As Nin described in the excerpt above, she dyed her hair in an effort to translate her appearance into reflecting who she felt she was on the inside. She felt like her coloring, an "indefinite" shade of blonde-red-brown, did not reflect her personality truly, but that black did.

To return to June Miller's dress, Nin often described June Miller's appearance as "shabby," but found her striking style a "wonder":

> What a profound joy to watch that crowd scurrying, and then to see her striding—resplendent—incredible, towards me. I cannot believe it. I hold her warm hand. She is going to call for mail. Doesn't the man see the wonder of her? Nobody like her ever called for mail at the American Express. Did any woman ever wear shabby shoes, a shabby black dress, a shabby dark blue cape and an old violet hat as she wore them? (Diary 32, p. 142)

> Then June came, all in black velvet, paler and more incandescent than ever… (Diary 32, p. 199)

> The ugly, unimaginative, dead people who surrounded us—We were blind to them. I looked at June, June incandescent on [*sic*, not "in"] black velvet.[10] (Diary 32, p. 201)

> Of your pallor, demoniac eyebrows, your cape, your barbaric jewelry, your erratic eating, impulses, your destruction of the boundary between day and night, your night prowling, your hatred of sunlight – all these I love. That you are Nastasia and Stavrogin I love. (Diary 32, p. 223)

After June Miller left Paris on January 19 or 20, 1932 (she sailed from Le Havre on January 20, 1932[11]), Nin herself wore a black velvet dress with holes at the elbows. Doing so reminded her of June Miller. In the first quote below, Nin's text is reproduced, including the word "elbows" she had crossed out before writing "sleeve," indicating that June's sleeves were at least long enough to extend below the elbow:

---

[10] In Nin (1986) this sentence reads "I look at June, in black velvet" (p. 32).
[11] Passenger and Crew Lists of Vessels Arriving at New York, New York, 1897-1957. Microfilm Publication T715, 8892 rolls. NAI: 300346. Records of the Immigration and Naturalization Service; National Archives at Washington, D.C. Year: 1932; Arrival: New York, New York; Microfilm Serial: T715, 1897-1957; Microfilm Roll: Roll 5103; Line: 19; Page Number: 132, retrieved from Ancestry.com, New York, Passenger Lists, 1820-1957 [database on-line]. Provo, UT, USA: Ancestry.com Operations, Inc., 2010.

> June had a hole in her ~~elbows~~ sleeve. [when they went to lunch on January 12, 1932] (Diary 32, p. 161)

> I had dressed very carelessly, and felt as if I were June. The dress I love best now is an old black velvet dress which is torn at the elbows. June's suit was torn at the elbows. (Diary 33, p. 22)

> I am happiest in my black velvet dress because it is old and has torn at the elbows. [from a letter to June Miller, copied into the diary] (Diary 33, p. 89)

In addition to dresses, Nin and June Miller also wore suits, which Nin sometimes referred to as "tailor" suits:

> We met the next day [January 12, 1932] at the American Express. She came in her tailor suit because I had said I liked it. (Diary 32, p. 160)

For Nin, however, a "tailor suit" was a rather plain thing to wear:

> I could almost wear an ordinary tailor suit now. (Diary 34, p. 301)

> Having a sense of my own value [now] I can wear a tailor suit without feeling effaced. (Diary 34, p. 301)

On a day in late June or July 1932, which she described as "luxuriant, tropical" (Diary 35, p.84), Nin wore what she called a "Scotch" suit, plus a hat and cape, indicating that the suit was most likely made of lighter weight fabric:

> He looked at me admiringly_ told me he loved my plain little Scotch suit..[two periods] …..At the end of our talk…I…put on my hat and cape… (Diary 35, pp. 84-85)

At home in Louveciennes with Henry Miller, with the house to themselves for a few days, Nin wore something quite different, as Miller described in a letter to Nin copied into the diary:

> I feel the greatest peace and joy sitting in the dining room listening to you rustling about, your dress like the goddess Indra studded with a thousand eyes. (Diary 35, pp. 202-203)

Nin described another dress worn at home with Henry Miller, one made of lace:

> I am lying on the bed. I wear a lace dress, nothing else, because it gives him pleasure to look at me. Now he says I look like an Ingres. (Diary 35, p.180)

Reflecting on her love of dress, compared to June Miller's bohemian shabbiness, Nin wrote:

> I know if I had been born on a farm…my peasant dress would be flowered cretonne, always washed & ironed… (Diary 32, p. 233)

> …a beautiful piece of material like Fortuny's means as much to me as a good book. (Diary 32, p. 234)

The rose dress mentioned previously was to make a few more appearances in the diaries, unless Nin had more than one of that color:

> I sit on his bed, with my wide rose dress spread around me, smoking, and he observes the spectacle. (Diary 33, p. 124)

> And I have barely kissed him [Hugh] goodbye, and the green gate is barely closed after him that I say to Emilia: clean my rose dress… (Diary 34, p.62)

> …I went to the kitchen in my stately rose dress. (Diary 34, p. 79)

> I was lying in bed—after dinner. Rose dress crumpled and stained. (Diary 34, pp. 176-177)

As Henry Miller recalled Nin's first visit to his hotel room in a letter to Nin (copied into the diary), he included the dress she wore that day in his description:

> Then I remember vividly your dress, the color and texture of it—precisely what I would have begged you to wear had I been able to anticipate the moment. (Diary 33, p. 127)

In the restaurant Les Vikings in Montparnasse with Eduardo Sanchez, Nin wore what she called a "Russian" ensemble:

> We sit in the mellow light…I wear a real Russian hat, and dress…(Diary 33, p. 153)

Dresses appeared in Nin's dreams, as well:

> March 19.   Dream: I wear a light airy pale green dress (the one I wore the day John kissed me in the hotel)… (Diary 33, p. 168)

In the summer of 1932, Nin described wearing a "very open" red lace blouse, plus having widened the necklines on her dresses. She was not entirely sure that this look corresponded with her nature, however:

> I have left my red blouse very open. My breasts show through the lace. Henry says: I love that. Open it more. (Entry dated June 15, 1932, Diary 35, p. 23)

> Leaving my blouse very open yesterday corresponds to a gesture I made about a month ago of slicing into my dresses with a large pair of scissors to widen the neckline[s].
> I do not mind whether or not this is a dissonance in my own nature. I believe dissonances are interesting. (Diary 35, p. 25)

Stockings

As for many women in the 1930s, stockings were of particular importance to Nin. The diaries included numerous mentions of her stockings, often black lace, and black silk garters.

> What I could have found ridiculous only touched me with its humanness: Henry crawling to find my black silk garters which had fallen behind the bed. (Diary 33, p. 132)

In an entry dated December 26, 1932, Nin mentioned that she did not "mind Banco's [the Guilers' large dog] paw marks on [her] stockings" (Diary 32, p.113). However, for the most part, stockings were an important and necessary part of her wardrobe, and one she would very much have minded having a dog's paw marks on. She included silk stockings in a list of "beautiful and good things" she considered necessary luxuries:

> I might be thrown into the slumps a hundred times and each time I would clamber out again to good coffee, on lacquered trays, by [p.233:] the side of an open fire. Each time I would clamber out to silk stockings and perfume. Absolute luxury is not a necessity to me, but beautiful and good things are. (Diary 32, pp. 232-233)

About June Miller's stockings in January 1932, Nin wrote: "I saw she wore ugly cotton stockings, and it hurt me to see June in cotton stockings (Diary 32, p.158)," and the word "ugly" does not appear in this passage in either Nin, 1966 or 1986. Like most upper-middle class women, Nin herself most likely wore sheer, silk stockings, like the pair she gave June Miller just before taking her shoe shopping, noted above. Sometimes these were lace, which Nin felt evoked the painting, "*Maja Desnuda*," by Francisco de Goya (a nude, whose partner painting, the "*Maja Vestida*," or "Clothed *Maja*" may be the painting actually Nin intended to reference):

> Feeling when June wore the open-work lacy black stockings I gave her, of the *Maja Desnuda* of Goya. (Diary 33, p. 71)

> ...or when I lay in the bed and he [Eduardo Sanchez] admired my Goyescan stockings... (Diary 33, p. 163)

Stockings were among the first articles of dress Henry Miller encouraged Nin to leave in his apartment for use during her overnight visits:

> Henry Miller: "Look, here is a drawer for your things _ _ It's so nice having a drawer full of your clothes—stockings." (Diary 34, p. 84)

Like many women of her time, Nin mended her stockings to make them last longer: "I see...a mend in my stockings" (Diary 34, p. 240). Sadly, one of the pairs that Nin had kept in Henry Miller's apartment was inadvertently gifted to a short-term house-guest, the underage girlfriend of his flatmate, Alfred (Fred) Perlès, much to Nin's anguish:

> He gave Paulette, out of soft heartedness, the pair of stockings I had left in his drawer—my best pair—while I was wearing mended stockings to save for gifts to him. (Diary 35, p. 211)

Nin clearly saw her stockings as part of a larger picture that included the rest of her dress as a whole and were even a part of her choice of setting for a romantic rendezvous with her cousin, Eduardo Sanchez:

> Isn't there art too in my choice of the [restaurant Les] Viking[s] with its mellow lights, nooks, dark wood walls and decorations of ships, in my Goyescan stockings, in every detail of my costume, in my divination of other's [sic] moods, in my surroundings, in my words__(Diary 33, p. 164)

June Miller, on the other hand, apparently went frequently without underwear or stockings, or wore cotton stockings, as Nin and Bald (1987) both described:

> I saw she wore ugly cotton stockings, and it hurt me to see June in cotton stockings. (Diary 32, p. 158)

> She was wearing a very light summer dress, and no stockings because she had no money for stockings… (Diary 32, p. 249)

> There is something inconsistent about a velvet cape, shantung dress and no stockings. (Bald, 1987)

Dick (1967) had hoped to write a biography of June Miller and interviewed her extensively, but instead included the material in his 1967 biography of Henry Miller. According to June Miller:

> "I never wore stockings, my legs were beautiful enough – if I couldn't afford the best stockings I wore none. In fact it was I who started the fashion for bare legs." (Dick, 1967, p. 120)

Shoes

Nin recorded having a variety of different kinds of shoes in the diaries. One of the more notable gifts Nin made to June Miller when she was visiting in Paris in January 1932 was a pair of sandals. First, June Miller expressed a shy admiration of Nin's sandals, saying that she had formerly worn sandals herself, but was unable to afford them at the moment. Nin offered to give her a pair that she had:

> She told me how at the restaurant, she had wanted to see my feet, and how she could not bring herself to stare – yet she wanted to see me.... She looked at my feet in the sandalled shoes, and thought them lovely..... I said: you like those sandals? She said: I always used to wear sandals, until I could no longer afford them. I said: Come up to my room and try the other pair I have. She tried them on, sitting on our bed. They were too small for her. (Diary 32, pp. 157-158)

Perhaps Nin's second pair of sandals were not Nin's size, and were already intended to be given as a gift. Nin made a gift of sandals to Hugh Guiler's sister, Ethel Guiler, "She wore my sandals..." (Diary 33, p. 201). Later, Nin took June Miller shoe shopping in Paris:

> ...she had promised to let me buy her the sandal shoes. (Diary 32, p. 150)

> We went to the shoe shop.....When they mentioned the broadness of June's feet I scolded them.......We chose the sandals. She refused anything else—an ordinary shoe—anything which was not symbolical or representative of me. Everything I wore she would wear, although she had never wanted to imitate anyone before. (Diary 32, pp. 164-165)

Nin also used the word "sandal" figuratively, when talking about the influence her relationship with Henry Miller had upon her sense of humor:

> Henry taught me to play. I had played before, in my own way, with a sandal-footed humor_ _ but his was like Tristan Tzara, "*une entreprise*

> *de demolition.*" It was lusty humor, and I have enjoyed it, to the point of hysteria… (Entry dated May 29, 1932, Diary 34, p. 269)

Nin wore sandals, even in Paris in January, and they were the topic of conversation between her and June Miller, but they were not the only type of footwear to receive mention in the diaries. Nin also wore a variety of other kinds of shoes:

> Will it seem strange to me someday….that my shoes are not shoes, but sandals, mocasins [sic], ballet slippers, espadrilles, or Russian boots? (Diary 32, p. 234)

> …[even] if I had been born on a farm… my shoes [would have been] of red linen… (Diary 32, p. 233)

> I observe my boots, my mocasins [sic] and my dressy shoes lined up regimentally in a corner of the room… (Diary 33, p. 9)

And, shoes made an appearance in a dream Nin described in the diary:

> I am frying eggs. I have two fried eggs inside of my shoe, resting on my toes. I walk with it slowly. I have very far to go. I'm afraid the egg will be cold before I get it to Henry. (Diary 34, p. 187)

Cosmetics: Lip Rouge, Powder, and Nail Polish

> Anaïs has an annoying habit of biting my ears with most affectionate intention. And of putting rouge on my lips, cheek, forehead, and neck; and powder on my coat-front. Tolerance is necessary to marriage. I tell myself this every morning when I find she has left the toothpaste open, and it is spreading over my shaving brush. (Journal of Hugh P. Guiler, p. 4[12])

---

[12] As with Nin's Diary 33 *Bis*, the pages of the Journal of Hugh P. Guiler were unnumbered by Guiler; when citing Guiler's journal, I refer to the pages by number, beginning with page 1 as the first page of text following the title page, on which the first entry, dated September 4 [1927], begins.

Nin described shopping for and wearing rouge and powder, and her husband Hugh Guiler's diary mentioned her use of powder and nail polish as well. Descriptions of Nin's cosmetics and fingernails also turned up in Dick's (1967) interviews with June Miller, in her impressions of Nin. June Miller's choices of colors in powder, rouge, and mascara were described in detail in Bald (1987) and received mention in Nin's journals; and more information appeared in lists of Henry Miller's observations of his wife which Nin copied into her journals. Each woman's make-up will be discussed in turn, beginning with Nin's.

Nin's Make-up

Nin and her husband Hugh Guiler described her having worn powder on her face and lip rouge on her lips. Nin also described her eye makeup as being "painted." After her whirlwind few weeks with June Miller in January 1932, Nin went away alone to Switzerland, where she wrote:

> Hotel Sonloup - Sonloup/Montreux, <u>Suisse</u>
> January 25 – After Henry's visit I began to tiger-pace the house and to say I had to go away. (Entry dated January 25, 1932, Diary 32, p. 217)

Feeling unsettled by her attachment to June Miller, admiring her husband's steadfastness, Nin wrote of how she had packed "hurriedly" and cared less for her appearance than usual:

> ...I made all the preparations—careless ones, unlike my usual self—I didn't care about appearances—clothes, etc. I came away hurriedly...[ellipse in text]
> > To find myself.
> > To find Hugh in myself.

Nin's uncharacteristic carelessness of dress on her way to Switzerland in late January included less make-up than usual, which was also intended to somehow "reassure" Hugh:

> An amusing incident in the train, going to Switzerland. To reassure Hugh I had not painted my eyes, barely powdered, barely rouged my lips, and not touched my nails. (Diary 33, p. 21)

She wondered at the effect of her appearance on a stranger on the train; so different from her usual look:

> He said, very nervously: Will you come and have coffee with me? I said no, and wanted to laugh because I was thinking: What would it have been if I had painted my eyes! (Diary 33, p. 22)

Later, while still in Switzerland, reflecting on the differences between her level of attention to dress and that of June Miller, Nin wrote:

> Will it seem strange to me someday…. That… my eyelashes [are] more heavily painted than a movie star… (Diary 32, p. 234)

By March 1932, once her affair with Henry Miller was underway, Nin wondered whether Henry Miller would make notes on her for use in his writing, as he did with his wife, June:

> Does he make such notes as: Anaïs:…..Indelible rouge. (Diary 33, p. 130)

Regarding her "indelible rouge," also wrote that Nin that she did not think her husband noticed when her rouge was smeared or she had stained her handkerchiefs with rouge, among other signs of intimate encounters with Henry and June Miller:

> The time I came back from Henry's room and washed myself, and he [Hugh] could have noticed…much rouge rubbed off on my handkerchief. (Diary 34, p. 27)
>
> The time after I kissed June when I saw the rouge spread unevenly about my mouth—he [Hugh] did not see… (Diary 34, p. 28)

Cosmetics were among the purchases Nin made at Printemps in Paris after having lunch with Eduardo Sanchez, after turning down his invitation to spend the rest of the afternoon together in a hotel room (Sanchez was adamant they spend the afternoon in a hotel room, whereas she suggested they see a movie, Diary 34, pp. 241-243), and having extra time to spend in Paris before an evening rendezvous with Henry Miller: "I buy rouge, powder, nail lacquer. I do not think of Eduardo" (Diary 34, p. 243).

Nail Polish

> Will it seem strange to me someday....That my nails do not look like nails but pearls? (Diary 32, p. 234)

> I want to write in colors too—my worship of color. I would like to write with the nacreous filament of my nails… (Diary 33, p. 55)

Nin often described her nail polish as being "nacreous" which would indicate that it was a pearlescent or shimmer polish. She believed it to be uncommon and it often made an appearance in her writing. This polish was even the topic of conversation when she and Hugh Guiler went to a house of prostitution for a private "exhibition," as both Nin and Guiler noted in their diaries. Before retiring to a private room for a paid performance by two prostitutes, Nin and Guiler were served drinks with the two women, who noticed Nin's nails. This turn in the conversation was noted by both Nin and Guiler in their diaries, and for Guiler was the "high moment of the evening" (Entry dated March 16, 1932, Journal of Hugh P. Guiler, p. 88):

> …I had the curious sensation of just sitting down for a social chat with two young ladies who had, like all Frenchwomen [sic][,] a gift for light conversation. It was all very civilized. The girls arched their fingers around their glasses….Then they noticed Anaïs' nails and said they liked the shell coloring she used on them—showed their own which were of the usual pink and said they preferred Anaïs's. How delightful was that seance of the finger nails! I shall never forget it. How simple & natural and feminine. Anaïs smiling at them—her madonna face smiling with sympathy and understanding. This was the real high moment of the evening. (Entry dated March 16, 1932, Journal of Hugh Guiler, pp. 87-88)

> I had not looked at their bodies but I had sensed them by their faces. We talk—oh, so politely. We discuss each other's nails; they comment on the unusualness of my nacreous nail polish… (Diary 33, p. 147)

Henry Miller also mentioned Nin's nail polish in a letter to Nin, the text of which she copied into the diary:

> I try to picture your life at Louveciennes but I can't……. Yes, I see the Poushkine [*sic*] legend clearly. I see you in my mind as sitting on that throne, jewels around your neck, sandals, big rings, painted finger nails… (Diary 33, p. 207)

In one entry, Nin purchased nail polish at Printemps in Paris, "I buy rouge, powder, nail lacquer" (Diary 34, p. 243). In another, Nin described her polished toe nails as being an object of fascination for Henry Miller: "This morning still, he was caressing wonderingly, the nacreous toe nails" (Diary 35, p. 185).

June Miller's Make-up

June Miller's "pallid" face has already been discussed above, which may have been due to her use of a light shade of powder. Wambly Bald in his weekly newspaper column, "La Vie de Bohème," called her "the girl with the golden face" (Bald, 1987, p. 91 [January 19, 1932] & p. 142 [July 25, 1933]).

> I was fascinated by her colorless face.
> "What kind of powder do you use?" I asked, with the cynicism of a journalist.
> "I am using Rachel No. 2," she answered, candidly. (Bald, 1987, [January 12, 1932] p. 87)

> June Mansfield, the girl with the golden face, is returning to New York. Over the blend of six shades of powder she paints futuristic designs on her face. Thus Montparnassed, June will pursue a movie contract. (Bald, 1987, [January 19, 1932] p. 91)

June Miller seemed to have worn a variety of shades of lip rouge, plus blue mascara:

Her lip rouge varies from all shades of red to green. Sometimes black......And her face—her face looks like the patina of some old coin, marked with eyelashes of midnight blue. (Bald, 1987, pp. 88-89)

June Miller's makeup and beauty practices, colorfully described in Bald (1987) above, were described in rather chaotic terms in both Nin's diaries and by Fred Perlès (Dick, 1967, p. 201). Nin wrote her impressions in the diaries and also copied Henry Miller's notes on June into Diary 33:

...her discolored mouth, badly rouged... (Diary 32, p. 136)

Medecine [sic] chest littered with cold cream jar, colored face powders, rouge sticks, shampoo oils, bleachers, castor oil, tweezers, blackhead removers, depilatories[,] etc. Visits to the beauty parlor spasmodically, next day same dirty finger nails! (Diary 33, pp. 60-61, from notes on June by Henry Miller, copied by Nin into the diary)

Magnificent June. Simple make up. Bloom of youth....
 [Greenwich] Village influence: bizarre make-up, use of dark powder, vaseline [sic] eyes, heavy mascara, grotesque decorations... (Diary 33, p. 112, from notes on June by Henry Miller, copied by Nin into the diary)

"Life in the flat was no longer bearable. Her things were all over the place...[ellipse in Dick's text] creams and cosmetics, bath salts and toilet waters...[ellipse in Dick's text] perfumes and powder puffs." (Perlès, as cited in Dick, 1967, p. 201)

Perfume

In her journals, Nin noted perfume as a part of her dress on various occasions. She wrote of wearing Mitsouko by Guerlain, Narcisse Noir by Caron, and Caron's *N'Aimez Que Moi* powder; Chypre by Coty appeared in a dream of Nin's as a bottle of holy water (Diary 35, pp. 243-244). In late 1931 and early 1932, Nin used her love of perfume as an example of her frivolous love of luxury:

> Nov.11-I cannot read a time table. I would rather buy a bottle of perfume than a book. I borrow the book. (Diary 32, pp. 53-54)

> I love good smells, cleanliness, health, elegance at the table... Perfume, for instance. What has perfume to say in communistic Russia. Taboo. We who are steering in the direction of a modified communism. What sacrifices I would make for a bottle of perfume. Incredible. I am so sound in other ways. I like simple food. I like inexpensive cigarettes. I abhor butlers, chauffeurs; a maid to dress me; *de luxe* suites on board a ship, all the show of autocratic [*sic*] living—I hate it. (Entry dated December 26, 1931, Diary 32, p. 113)

> I might be thrown into the slumps a hundred times and each time I would clamber out again to good coffee, on lacquered trays, by the side of an open fire. Each time I would clamber out to silk stockings and perfume. (Diary 32, pp. 232-233)

Not long after Nin wrote those words, perfume was to figure heavily in her relationship with June Miller. June Miller had noticed the scent in the Guilers' home and asked for Nin's perfume when Nin said she wanted to give her a going away present:

> When I tell her I want to give her a going away present she says she wants some of that perfume she smelled in my house—to evoke memories. (Diary 32, p. 147)

> And she has kept that incredible, out of date, uncallous sentimentalism: give me the perfume I smelled in your house. (Diary 32, p. 150)

Perfume was one of the gifts of clothing and accessories that Nin made to June Miller:

> We met the next day [January 12, 1932] at the American Express....She had said she wanted nothing from me but the perfume I wore, and my wine colored handkerchief....I made her go to the Ladies room. I opened my bag. (Diary 32, p. 160)

Interestingly, both published editions of this passage (Nin, 1966, p. 31 & Nin, 1986, p. 23) say Nin opened "*a* bottle of perfume," but if Nin were giving June Miller the perfume she had said she wanted, "the bottle," as it appears in Diary 32, p. 161 ("Meanwhile I opened the [*sic*] bottle of perfume. 'Put some on'" (Diary 32, p. 161)), makes much more sense—more sense than the idea of Nin carrying around a bottle of perfume that can be opened (as she did not describe using an atomizer to spray the perfume) and could potentially have leaked in her handbag. As for why Nin wanted her to wear the perfume immediately, the diary had no mention of whether June Miller smelled too unpleasant to go out with, and no mentions of her scent or odor appeared in the diaries examined in this study. Nin may simply have been giving June Miller the gifts of the perfume and stockings at that moment because it was the most convenient time and place to do so before heading to lunch together. Later, Nin noted that June Miller had been known to wash laundry in order to be able to afford perfume, so perhaps she simply felt that to be able to wear the perfume as soon as possible would be very important to June: "…June who washes laundry to pay [*sic*] for herself a bit of perfume…" (Diary 32, p. 169).

Perfume figured further in the two women's conversations, as Nin discovered not long after this that June Miller had spent half the 400 francs she had given the Millers' to buy food with (supposed to have been enough to last them a month, Nin, 1966, p. 39) on perfume instead:

> At lunch we were talking about perfumes, their substance, their mixture, their meaning. She said casually—Saturday, when I left you, I bought some perfume for Ray – (Ray is a girl she has told me about.) At the moment I did not think. I retained the name. It was a very expensive perfume. (Diary 32, pp. 189-190)

> She was telling me that she and Henry had quarreled over buying butter. They had no money and——No money, I said, but Saturday I gave you 400 frs for you and Henry to eat with – and today is Monday. "We had things to pay back up that we owed - -["] I thought she meant their hotel room. Then suddenly I remembered the perfume which cost 200 frs. Why didn't she say to me: I bought perfume and gloves and stockings Saturday? She didn't look at me when she intimated they had back rent to pay. (Diary 32, p. 196)

In a two-column list of her two natures (the "Abstract" and the "Human"), Nin included "love of fine smells" (Diary 33, p. 23) and "any sacrifice for perfume" (Diary 33, p. 24). In a list of things her husband had done for her, for which she was grateful ("What Hugh has done for me"), Nin wrote: "Never buys clothes for himself but buys me perfumes" (Diary 33, p. 38). The diaries also revealed that Nin liked to apply perfume to her hair, and that her hairdresser did this for her as well:

> I perfume my black hair now. (Diary 33, p. 49)

> The coiffeur…made love to me the other day. He poured a small bottle of perfume over me… (Diary 35, p. 244)

> …the hairdresser saved all the bits of perfume in the bottles to pour over my hair as a gift… (Diary 36, p. 150)

Perfume also made an appearance in the diaries in relation to Henry Miller's, Fred Perlès's, and Eduardo Sanchez's responses to Nin's dress. When in a hotel room with Sanchez, he complimented Nin and she used the word "perfume" when describing his admiration:

> His compliments were very ordinary: velvet eyes, defiant breasts, body like a reed, perfume of my flesh… (Diary 33, p. 158)

She noticed the effect of her perfume on Sanchez at other times, as well:

> We walk together very close. We are half-sad, half-joyous. It is warm. He smells my perfume. I look at his beautiful face. We desire each other….[four periods] But it's a mirage. It's only a gust_because we are young, and it is summer—and we are walking body against body. (Diary 34, pp. 207-208)

> Eduardo is drugged. I seduce him. With words, perfume (Narcisse Noir)[,] fallings of my head towards him, duel with eyes, and mouth and pressure of elbows… (Diary 34, p. 212)

Perfume made an appearance in Henry Miller's stories to Nin about his bohemian life with June in New York City:

> ...June buying perfume while Henry starved, or taking pleasure in concealing a bottle of old Madeira in her trunk while Henry and his friends, penniless, wished desperately for something to drink. (Diary 33, p. 290)

Around this time, Miller expressed that he enjoyed the lingering scent of her perfume in his apartment in Clichy:

> "Anaïs, when I came home last night I thought you were here, because I smelled your perfume. I missed you. I realize I didn't tell you at the moment, when you were here, how wonderful it was to have you here..[two periods] I never say those things well..[two periods] Look, here is a drawer for your things _ _ It's so nice having a drawer full of your clothes—stockings. I want you to leave your perfume all through the place..." Diary 34, p. 84)

Perfume then became one of the essentials Nin kept at Henry Miller's apartment for her overnight visits:

> I have left my pyjama[s][*sic*], comb, powder, perfume, in Henry[']s room. (Diary 34, p. 64)

Of the perfumes that were mentioned by name in the diaries, Guerlain's Mitsouko and Caron's Narcisse Noir, were the two which appeared most often. Nin described Miller as preferring Narcisse Noir, while his flatmate, Fred Perlès, preferred Mitsouko. At first, Henry Miller's dislike of Mitsouko hurt Nin's feelings:

> Henry is toughening me. When I come and find out that he doesn't like my perfume because it is too delicate—at first I am a bit hurt. Fred loves Mitsiku [*sic*], but Henry likes acrid powerful perfumes…[ellipse] He always demands assertion, potency. And some part of my own being responds to Henry's demands..[two periods] After a moment I am glad Henry has called for the more potent perfume, as if he called out potency from me. Mitsiku [*sic*] appears faint. (Diary 34, pp. 170-171)

> Fred and I are bantering. "Fred, after I spend a week with Henry, I'll spend two days with you—in a hotel—so I can take Henry there. He loves to be taken to hotels where I have been before. Two days."
>
> "We'll have breakfast in bed. Mitsiku [*sic*] perfume. A chic hotel. Yes?" (Diary 34, pp. 196-197)

These two perfumes made another appearance in Nin's journal, in the form of a metaphorical substitute for the colored inks Nin sometimes wrote with, and evocative of other scents from nature she wished to capture in her diary as she recorded some of the more intimate details of her lived experience:

> "Have you enough heliotrope ink?" Henry asked. I should not be using ink but perfume. I should be writing with Narcisse Noir, with Mitsiku [*sic*], and jasmin [*sic*], with amber and honeysuckle. I would write beautiful words which would exale [*sic*] a potent smell of woman's honey and the man's white blood. And rain. (Diary 34, p. 237)

Nin also included perfume in a list of beautiful things she admired when shopping in Printemps in Paris, after just having rejected Eduardo Sanchez. She refused to "sacrifice" herself for his desire for her, but acknowledged herself to be a "slave…of [her] desires" for a list of articles of dress that included perfume:

> I see him walking aimlessly and desolately. I am quite hard, and quite indifferent. No more sacrifices. No more selflessness. I cross the street and walk into the Printemps. (Diary 34, p. 242)

> I would like to be naked and cover myself with cold crystal jewelry. Jewelry and perfume………I am the slave of …Of my desires for perfume and jewelry. (Diary 34, p. 243)

Nin also gave part of the packaging of her *N'Aimez Que Moi* (translation: "love no one but me") powder by Caron to Henry Miller:

> I cut out the top of my box of powder with the name of the powder on it: "*N'Aimez Que Moi*, Caron, Rue de la Paix"! He carries this in his vest pocket. (Diary 34, p. 265)

Because this was the name of one of Caron's perfumes, this was more likely a scented body powder, rather than facial powder. Chypre, by Coty appeared in a dream of Nin's, in the form of a bottle of holy water:

> There is a round communion table—yes. People walk to it with folded hands, but smiling. You are given a small bottle of holy water which you must drink. As I take mine I see it is a small bottle of Chypre perfume. I smell it and instead of drinking it I pour it over myself. I am extremely elated. (Diary 35, pp. 243-244)

Nin also included perfume in lists of things that she shopped for, in her attempt at "originality," as a woman who took "puerile joy" in "trivialities related to dressing," and used shopping to "run away from [her] moods":

> Plan for Absolute Originality [at top of page, like a title]
> [blank line]
> I cannot plan for it. It comes unexpectedly, when I am choosing writing papers, a pair of shoes, an ash tray, a perfume, a Christmas card, a bottle of ink, a material for a dress. (Diary 36, p. 6)

> But I am running away from myself until tomorrow when I see Allendy and Henry! Play my usual trick of going shopping, going on errands to luxurious places, basking in trivialities all related to dressing, embellishment etc. What symbolism in the quest for perfume, powder—a new handbag, new gloves—the puerile joy of the woman! (Entry dated September 21, 1932, Diary 36, p. 108)

> How do I run away from my own moods—and where? The cave of rock crystal, the pure delight of sensual beauty in silk velvet, furs, perfumes, colors, glassware, I wander through the shops as through wonder… (Entry dated "September," Diary 36, p. 129)

The Scent of the Diaries

As field notes from visits to UCLA reflected, one of the first sensory impressions in examining Nin's leather-covered, hand-written diaries was their scent. The diaries from the 1920s through the 1930s all have a scent initially interpreted as a heavy, spicy, floral incense. This scent immediately brought to mind the following: "Horace brought me incense from Greece" (Entry dated Tuesday, November 9, 1927[13], Nin, 1985, p. 32). My first thought was that the diaries had the scent because Nin had burned incense in her home. The diaries recorded that Nin had smoked cigarettes and her husband had smoked a pipe, but unlike papers or belongings from a heavy tobacco smoker, either cigarettes or a pipe, the diaries did *not* smell like tobacco smoke. Neither do the diaries smell like books that have been shelved in a library for nearly fifty years.

Internet searches for "Narcisse Noir" revealed that the perfume dates from 1911 and is still in production. It is made by the house of Caron, and was supposedly a favorite of Gloria Swanson and Dita von Teese. Fragrantica.com, an online "perfume encyclopedia" classed Narcisse Noir as an Oriental floral and identified the top, middle and base notes: "Top notes are african [*sic*] orange flower and narcissus; middle notes are jasmine, orange and tincture of rose; base notes are vetyver [*sic*], musk and sandalwood" (Fragrantica, n.d.) Online reviews of the perfume on Basenotes.net, Fragrantica, and Perfume Emporium, described Narcisse Noir as orangey, grapey, and smokey, some even describing it as smelling dusty, and like incense and old leather. A vintage sample of Narcisse Noir and a new bottle of Mitsouko were purchased for this study. The 2 ml sample of Narcisse Noir, decanted from a vintage bottle, was purchased from a seller on Etsy.com. Its scent was compared to the description of the diaries' scent in my field notes and to descriptions of the scent in online reviews. One online reviewer (Basenotes, n.d.) described Narcisse Noir as smelling like grape-flavored Kool-Aid brand powdered drink mix. To my nose, the top notes are reminiscent of the wildflower sky lupine (*Lupinus nanus*). To some, this variety of lupine smells reminiscent of artificial grape flavoring, which could reasonably be expected to be similar to the scent of grape-flavored Kool-Aid. This similarity between my interpretation of the scent and the online reviewer's served to establish the validity of online reviews in describing the scent of Narcisse Noir. This validity further established that the 2 ml vintage sample was an accurate sample of what the perfume should smell like. After about an hour of wearing, the scent dried down to smell like leather and old paper, which are also component scents of the diaries in UCLA, being that many of them have leather covers. The diaries did not smell exactly like Narcisse Noir, but their scent had many elements in common with the vintage sample.

---

[13] Also found on the opening page of manuscript Diary 25 (p. 1).

The question *why* the hand-written diary books would be so heavily scented, and with such staying power may be answered thus: As described above, the diaries do *not* smell like they have been in library storage for decades. They smell like someone's home, like perfume and incense, and being leather bound books, they naturally smell of old leather and old paper. Nin may have deliberately scented the books with perfume herself, and she may have worn a more lasting and concentrated formulation of the perfume than is available nowadays. Or, she may simply have applied her perfume to the insides of her wrists, where it rubbed off onto the pages of the diary as she wrote.

Hairstyling

As discussed previously, it was recorded in the diary that Nin dyed her hair black in January 1932:

> Will it seem strange to me someday....That my hair is now blacker than a raven's...(Diary 32, p. 234)

> [In a list of things Hugh did for her that she appreciated:] Lets me dye my hair. (Diary 33, p. 38)

> I want to write in colors too—my worship of color. I would like to write... with the black of my hair... (Diary 33, p. 55)

Whether she maintained the color or not was not found. She seemed to have preferred a comb with which to style her hair, rather than a brush.

> ...to comb my hair,... (Diary 33, p. 128)

> I had been standing before the mirror combing my hair. (Diary 33, p. 162)

One of Nin's combs was green, and even though it had broken in half, she continued to use it:

> My green comb broke in two. I keep half of it for Ruby's [her dog] white hair, and half for my black hair, side by side. (Entry dated February 3, 1932, Diary 33, p. 9)

> Does he make such notes as: Anaïs: —green comb with black hair on… (Diary 33, p. 130)

The "Journal[s] of Facts" present at the backs of some of the diaries reflect regular visits to the hairdresser. Nin's writings in which she mentioned her hair generally referred to her combing her hair or styling it in a way that looked "wild" or "Grecian":

> Intelligence—perhaps at last emotionless (I always thought if it were not for the feelings which make me a dupe, an idiot, a saint) Defiantly I pin my hair up on top of my head. Tonight I dominate the world. I love these moments on the captain's watch tower: they are so rare. (Diary 33, p. 287)

> …Henry liking to find hairpins on the floor of his room because hairpins on the floor evoke wildness… (Diary 34, p. 166)

> It is like when he asked me to change my hair because he likes wildness in hair. When he uttered the word wildness I responded to it _ _ yes, yes, like something I have been wanting obscurely_ _ Wild hair. His hands through my hair—always his stocky firm hands through my hair. My hair is in his mouth when we sleep. And when I throw myself back on my chair and put my two hands clasped behind my head, raising my hair, in a Grecian way, he exclaims: that is the way I like it. (Diary 34, pp. 171-172)

> [when attending her brother Joaquín's debut concert:] …wild hair… (Diary 34, p. 208)

As noted previously, after lunching with her cousin Eduardo Sanchez one afternoon, Nin decided to fill her free time by going shopping at Paris's famous department store, Printemps. She purchased make-up, nail polish and jewelry, and then went to a salon to have her hair done, where she began to write in the diary as she sat there:

> <u>At</u> <u>the</u> <u>coiffeur</u>. <u>Under</u> <u>the</u> <u>hot</u>-<u>air</u> <u>coffer</u>. Why the coiffeur? And Eduardo walking aimlessly away. We were going to spend the whole afternoon together. (Diary 34, p. 241)

Jewelry

"She wore her jewelry with exquisitely good taste," said June Miller of Nin (Dick, 1967, p. 199). Jewelry was another important part of Nin's dress and appearance that received mention in the diaries. Early in the period addressed by this study, Nin wrote of how she gifted jewelry to June Miller. Dick (1967) described this as "a sign of going steady":

> …Anais pinned June by giving her coral earrings and a turquoise ring. (Dick, 1967, p. 117)

Although Nin's husband was a banker and they socialized with "society," she did not mention having a great deal of jewelry or jewelry that was made of precious stones and metals. Nin either did not own fine jewelry or simply did not afford it much attention when writing. She was familiar with the Florence's Ponte Vecchio, probably from having visited Florence with Hugh several years prior, and in 1932 wrote:

> …I would still prefer the Bridge of Jewelry in Florence to most of its museums… (Diary 32, p. 234)

Those items of jewelry that received specific mention were a turquoise ring, a pair of coral earrings, June's silver bracelet given to Nin, "barbaric" jewelry worn by both women, a necklace given to one of Hugh's sisters, and large rings worn by Nin. Nin gave to Hugh's sister Ethel Guiler her "favorite necklace" in "punishment for [her] inordinate love for costume and ornament" (Diary 32, p. 35). The primary gifts Nin made to June Miller were in the form of jewelry and accessories, and as described earlier, Nin gave her stockings, perfume, and sandals. The day they went shoe shopping, January 12, 1932, Nin took her to lunch, but not before insisting she wear perfume and sheer stockings, instead of her usual (cotton, or none at all) (Diary 32, pp. 160-161, "Journal of Facts," n.pag.). Appropriately perfumed and stockinged, the two women then went to lunch and ate seated side by side, where Nin gave June Miller more gifts before going shopping for sandals like Nin's (in Paris, in mid-January). Nin gave her a pair of coral earrings and a ring she found painful to part with:

> And not knowing what else to say I spread on the bench, between her and me, the wine colored handkerchief she wanted, my coral earrings which she had looked for in shops, my turquoise green ring which Hugh had given me and which it hurt me to give, but it was blood I wanted to lay before June's beauty, and now before June's incredible humility. She talked then beautifully, not hysterically and anecdotally—deeply. (Diary 32, pp. 163-164)

Nin seemed to have ascribed a change in June Miller's conversation style (from "hysterically" to "beautifully") that came about as a result of having received these gifts from Nin. Interestingly, the words "which she had looked for in shops" do not appear in the published versions of the above passages in Nin (1966 & 1986). Not long after this, June Miller gave Nin her "only bracelet" (Diary 33, p. 182) on January 16, 1932, the same day Nin had her hair dyed black (Diary 32, p. 178 & "Journal of Facts," n.pag.). Nin's husband, Hugh, was not pleased to see his wife wearing this bracelet, but Nin attached deep meaning to the gift. When he pretended to take it away from her, to "tease" her, she first resisted, and then caved, knowing he would not really be so unkind as to keep it:

> ...she gave me her very own silver bracelet with a cat's eye stone—so symbolical of her—when she has so few possessions. I refused at first, and then the joy of wearing her bracelet, a part of her, filled me. I carry it like a symbol. It is precious to me. Hugh noticed it and hated it. He wanted to take it from me, to tease [*sic*] me. I held on to it while he crushed my hands—with all my strength. Then he let go—he looked hurt. Then I offered it to him because I will never hurt him. Yielding again—perhaps this time not very sincerely because I knew he would not deprive me of it. That is his way. (Diary 32, p. 178)

Later, Nin wrote of how she told June how much wearing her bracelet meant to her:

> I told her how her bracelet clutched my wrist like her very fingers, held me in barbaric slavery. (Diary 32, p. 190)

Nin even granted June's bracelet the status of "talisman" and described in a letter to June, the text of which she copied into her diary, how the effect of wearing June's bracelet was such that she cared less for Henry than she did for keeping what she perceived as June's shared romantic feelings a secret from Henry:

> I wear your bracelet like a talisman. Since I have worn it many things [p.89:] to which I attached great value mean less to me. Henry's talent, genius, knowledge—I am willing to lose them for the sake of keeping our feeling a secret from him. (Diary 33, pp. 88-89)

Later, as the Millers' marriage came to an end, the two women exchanged their gifts of jewelry. June Miller's side of the story is below:

> "As for the coral earrings and the turquoise ring I gave them back to her and I retrieved my silver bracelet with the cat's-eye stone." (June Miller, in Dick, 1967, p. 120)

> "The only thing Anais gave me", said June, "was a blue stone ring and a shabby cape. I gave her a silver cat's-eye stone bracelet and when I left her in anger I gave her back her ring and took my bracelet because I wanted nothing of hers and did not want her to have anything of mine." (Dick, 1967, p. 162)

Nin had written in the diary that she was in fact "ready to give [June Miller] everything I have ever invented & created, from my house, my costumes, my jewelry…" (Diary 33, p. 74). Having already given a necklace to her sister-in-law Ethel Guiler, Nin wrote this gifting of things she enjoyed was symbolic and, like June's bracelet, she perceived those gifts to have some ability to affect the wearer in some way:

> Observe symbolism in my gift of jewelry to Ethel [sister-in-law] and then to June. (Diary 33, p. 29)

> My influence on Ethel in N.Y. She not only wore my necklace, but she reawakened herself to new moods: she sat in her room and cried with unknown feelings. (Diary 33, pp. 201-202)

A 12-franc necklace that Nin wore when visiting Henry Miller's hotel room was described as "barbaric," and she was bemused that he found it precious:

> What I could have found ridiculous only touched me with its humanness…His awe before my 12 francs necklace: It is such a fine, rare thing you wear. (Diary 33, p. 132)

> Does he make such notes as: Anaïs: ….. Barbaric necklace. Breakable. Fragile. (Diary 33, p. 130)

> …in his bed, naked, with my barbaric jewelry tinkling… (Diary 33, p. 131)

Further into their affair, and following the publication of her book on D. H. Lawrence (Nin, 1932), Nin wrote to Henry Miller of her conservative, Cuban family's resultant shame and disappointment, and described herself as having been viewed by her family as some kind of Alexander Pushkin-inspired legendary figure who had disillusioned them:

> You see, I had been carved on copper and set with jewels for a legend of Poushkin [*sic*]… (Diary 33, p. 192)

Henry Miller wrote back, in a letter the text of which was transcribed into her journal, and jewels, including "big rings," figured in his description:

> Yes, I see the Poushkine [*sic*] legend clearly. I see you in my mind as sitting on that throne, jewels around your neck, sandals, big rings, painted finger nails, strange Spanish voice, living some kind of a lie which is not a lie exactly but a fairytale… (Diary 33, p. 207)

In addition to rings and necklaces, Nin also wore a wristwatch. It appeared in her journal as a reminder of her husband, and the awareness that she could not stay overnight at Henry Miller's apartment and would soon have to return home:

> My watch is pulsing tyrannically against my pulse…It clasps my wrist like two of Hugh's long fingers and makes me aware of the end of our evening, of the ephemeralness of my sitting there between Henry and Fred. (Diary 34, p. 8)

In the summer of 1932, Nin purchased a pair of steel bracelets from Printemps in Paris. As described previously, she had done this shopping when she found herself with extra time to fill before an evening meeting with Henry Miller. Nin first wrote that she purchased one steel bracelet, but in later entries, described having purchased a pair and how to her, they were like a pair of handcuffs. She wrote of herself as a "slave" to her desires for jewels and perfume, but also her unwillingness to be subject to Sanchez's desire for her (Diary 34, pp. 242-243). Nin saw a connection between her attraction to the strength of the steel, the hardness of the rocks and crystals on display with the jewelry in Printemps, and her new strength to resist her cousin's manipulation:

> I see him [Sanchez] walking aimlessly and desolately. I am quite hard, and quite indifferent. No more sacrifices. No more selflessness. I cross the street and walk into the Printemps. I go to the necklaces and bracelets and ear-rings which dazzle me always. Jewelry. I stand like a bewildered and fascinated savage. Joy. Glitter. Sheen. Amethyst. Steel. Turquoise. Shell pink. Irish green. I would like to be naked and cover myself with cold crystal jewelry. Jewelry and perfume. The rocks from which the stones are cut are exposed in show-windows [sic]. The frozen bulk of color, works insidiously on my mind. I see a very broad flat steel bracelet. Heavy, inflexible. Hand-cuffs. Siberia. I am the slave of a bracelet. Of my desires for perfume and jewelry. The bracelet is clasped on my wrist. I pay....I do not think of Eduardo. I come to the coiffeur, where I can sit still and frozen like rock crystal. I write with a wrist encircled in steel. Symbols. Indestructability. Crystallization of softness. Steel. Crystallization. (Diary 34, pp. 242-243)

Nin discussed the steel bracelets with her psychoanalyst, Dr. Allendy, reflecting on the deeper meaning behind her purchase. Dr. Allendy believed the purchase to be related to feelings of guilt for rejecting Sanchez that afternoon and for being unfaithful to her husband. Nin did not agree with his interpretation, however:

> He [Allendy] is confused by what I tell him about Eduardo, about wanting to be cruel to Hugh the same day, and about the bracelets, and my not being cruel to Henry. (Entry dated May 27, 1932, 8th visit to Dr. Allendy, Diary 34, p. 249)

> Allendy did not understand the bracelets. I bought two of them, he says, in contradiction to my feeling of satisfaction at hurting Eduardo and Hugh (in intuition)[.] As soon as I achieve cruelty, I want at the same time to prostrate myself. One bracelet for Eduardo and one for Hugh.
> This I do not believe. I chose the two bracelets with a feeling of absolute subjection to Henry and liberation from the tenderness which binds me to Eduardo and Hugh. When I showed them to Henry I stretched out both my wrists as one does when one is being handcuffed. It seemed to me I was prostrating myself before Henry, wishing to be subjected. (Diary 34, pp. 250-251)

To Nin, the steel bracelets symbolized both a new-found inner strength, liberating her from Eduardo and her husband, and a feeling of being bonded only to Henry Miller. She saw herself as both a slave to her love of jewelry and her love for Henry Miller. Later, Nin dreamt she was wearing gems and admired for being a beautiful statue, but not human:

> I stood in dark space, dressed luxuriously in brocades and jewels, like a Byzantine idol. I wore a tiara of precious stones. I stood like an idol. People said: "She is a resplendent idol but not a human being." (Diary 35, p. 69)

Undergarments

Of all Nin's articles of clothing mentioned in her diaries, underclothes, particularly those made of black lace, were mentioned nearly as often as dresses. Unfortunately, she did not describe these garments in great detail, and left no indication whether these were brassieres, drawers/bloomers, panty briefs, or slips. However, she often mentioned that her undergarments were "black lace," seeming to include them to punctuate her diary entries with sensual detail:

> While I was away he [Hugh] found my black lace underwear, and he kissed it and he found the odor of me, and inhaled it with such joy. (Diary 33, p. 20)

While I was away he found my black lace underwear, and he kissed it and he found my odor, and slept with it. (Entry dated February 16, 1932, Diary 33 *Bis*, p. 2)

I am amazed at my lying there in his [Henry Miller's] iron bed, with my black underwear vanquished and trampled. (Diary 33, p. 117)

To the investigator I offer enigmatic replies.
    When I was dressing I was laughingly commenting on my underwear, on my wearing clothes which June had liked, June who is always naked..[two periods] It is Spanish, I said.
    Henry said: What comes to my mind when you say this is how did June know that you wore such clothing?
    I said: ["]Don't think I am trying to make it all more innocent than it was—but at the same time, don't go so directly at ideas like that or you'll never get quite the truth." (Diary 33, pp. 140-141)

Is it I slipping off my clothes before Eduardo—Eduardo and I loaded down, suffocated with terror of great moments! Great moments? In the yellow darkness, I lie on the large bed with utter ease..[two periods] and Eduardo, become another, takes off the last black lace piece and is moved by the revelation of my young breasts…[AN's ellipse] (Diary 33, pp. 157-158)

And I have barely kissed him [Hugh] goodbye, and the green gate is barely closed after him that I say to Emilia: clean my rose dress and wash my lace underwear—I may go and visit a friend for a few days. (Diary 34, p. 62)

Impulsively, swiftly I came to the bed, sat very near him, put my face very near his _ my coat slipped off, and the straps of my chemise too… (Diary 33, p. 162)

In my bedroom I take off a [*sic*] stained underwear. (Diary 34, p. 175)

Although this study did not analyze the works of Henry Miller, according to the diary Nin's black lace underwear made an appearance his writing as well:

> ...that morning the dawn caught us talking, and Henry and I fell on his bed exhausted, but he was still talking deliriously about the strainer which was thrown by mistake in the water closet, black lace underwear, and coral, etc out of which he wrote afterwards that inimitable parody of my novel. (Diary 34, p. 269, entry dated May 29, 1932)

June Miller, apparently, was known for going without underwear:

> So she took my hand against her warm breast, and we walked, I feeling her hand on her breast, under her dress, with no underwear between her body and the dress. (Diary 32, p. 194.)

Underwear appeared to have been among the things June Miller asked Nin for directly, or at the very least, was obviously in need of:

> When I tell her I want to give her a going away present she says she wants some of that perfume she smelled in my house—to evoke memories. And she needs shoes, stockings, gloves, underwear! (Diary 32, p. 147)

Evening Dresses

Evening dresses were one of the things Nin probably purchased from a dressmaker. As her affair with Henry Miller became more intense, she noted that her husband had discovered she been neglecting the housekeeping and, among other concerns, had missed a fitting for a gown:

> Hugh has found out that:
> I have not seen the gardener about the garden
> the mason about the cracked pool
> have not done my accounts
> have not taken my picures [*sic*]
> have missed my *essayage* for evening dress
> broken all routine. (Entry dated May 7, 1932, Diary 34, pp. 140-141)

One particularly notable event was Nin's brother Joaquín Nin-Culmell's debut concert. Nin described in detail her experience as she was dressed up for the occasion. When her brother made his debut as a pianist and composer, Nin felt vulnerable and on display when attending the concert and going to a café with her family afterward. She was intensely aware of the gaze of others on this occasion, as an upper-middle class woman in evening dress, as the daughter of a concert pianist, as the sister of the star of the evening, and as the wife of the man who financed her brother's music education. Nin's father's appearance at the concert was unexpected, and upsetting, for he had been estranged from his children for years, and he initially positioned himself at the entrance to the concert, greeting arriving guests as if he were the patron of the event. Nin had invited Dr. Allendy and Henry Miller (who brought his friend Michael Fraenkel) to the concert, for her own moral support, and included her perceptions of how they interpreted her appearance in her description of the event, as well as the effect her appearance had on her cousin, Eduardo Sanchez. She began by describing herself as making a beautiful impression that belied her internal discomfort; in the end, she described herself as a woman surrounded by a handful of male admirers. She was aware of her dress, her walk, voice, gestures, and their effects on others and described her experience in the passages below:

> The Concert. Poor Joaquin nervous at first. Eduardo sitting next to me. I in a magnificent, incredible Persian lamé dress—wild hair—
> …..As I walk about with feline movements, I know I am seducing every body [*sic*]. (Diary 33 *Bis*, p. 108)

> The concert. Eduardo sitting next to me—so beautiful. I in a magnificent, incredible Persian lamé dress—wild hair—beautiful with happiness, excitement. My lover Henry sitting where I cannot see him….. As I walk about in feline, seductive movements I know I am seducing Allendy, and Eduardo, and Henry, and many others. There was a very handsome Italian violinist_ _ There was my Father who changed his seat to place himself in front of me_ _ _ There was a Spanish painter_ _ others. One layer of physical confidence, in gestures and attitudes. One layer of timid seductiveness. One layer of confidence in the loves I have. One layer of childish terror and despair because Mother made such a scene when she saw Father arriving at the concert_ _ …..

> Henry was intimidated by the crowd. Soft and timid. He is like me: he is soft and timid.... So many layers. Aphone [*sic*] voice. Impossible face. Graceful walk. Fear of the crowd, fatigue at the talk and greetings. Statue like poise before my Father. Mixture. The child is still frightened, while the woman radiates beauty...... (Diary 34, pp. 208-210)

> I feel soft and so gentle that I don't know how the others' [*sic*] notice me. And they do. I gave the impression of beauty last night. I saw it in many eyes. I saw it in Joaquin's eyes. I don't want to be aware of all these layers walking about softly with me. I carry layers of feelings. Sensations. The heavy lamé on my naked body. The caress of the velvet cape. The weight of the full sleeves. The hypnotic glow of the lights. Do my eyes stare? I do not feel them blinking. I am walking seductively through a full concert hall. I am aware of my trailing walk. Of hands shaking mine. Of compliments. (Diary 34, pp. 210-211)

> Eduardo is drugged. I seduce him. With words, perfume (Narcisse Noir) fallings of my head towards him, duel with eyes, and mouth and pressure of elbows and the pressure of what we divine in each others [*sic*]. He divines my coquetry and my confidence. <u>My Eduardo.</u> ...... In the car Eduardo's leg seeks mine. Joaquin covers me with his cape. Joaquin loves me. I pressed Henry's hand very hard. Soft, timid. I understand all this—while I walked so confidently my real self was trembling. The ordeal of many people looking and talking. You have to play a comedy. I play a comedy. As I enter the café [*sic*] du Rond Point everybody looks at me. I see I have fooled them. I have concealed the smaller me. People are conscious of Joaquin and me—persons—They whisper as they look at us. Mother looks like a market woman praising her fresh vegetables. (Diary 34, pp. 212-213)

Nin also recorded Henry Miller's impression of her bearing and appearance, as written in a letter to her, which she transcribed into her journal:

> You stood there like a Princess. <u>You</u> were the <u>Infanta</u>! You looked thoroly [*sic*] disappointed in me. What was the matter? Did I look

stupid [?] (His lack of confidence!) I probably was. I wanted to get down on my knees and kiss the hem of your dress. So many Anaïses you have shown me—and now this one! – as if to prove your protean versatility. Do you know what Fraenkel said to me? "I never expected to see a woman of such femininity, such beauty, write a book like that?" Oh, that pleased me no end! The little tuft of hair coming up over the crown, the lustrous eyes, the georgeous [sic] shoulder line, - and those sleeves I adore, regal, Florentine, diabolistic! I saw nothing below the bosom. I was too excited to stand off and survey you. How much I [p.223:] wanted to whisk you away forever. Eloping with the Infanta—ye gods. (Diary 34, pp. 222-223)

Nin's lamé dress and other evening dresses appeared in her dreams, as well:

I am at a party. My beautiful lamé dress catches on everything and I tear it off. I can't walk. (Diary 34, pp. 185-186)

Dream. I am in a ball—beautifully dressed. It is the King who wants to dance with me, and who loves me. He whispers loving phrases in my ear. I am terrifically happy and I laugh a great deal. I dance alone before everybody. I am driving in a carriage, with my enormous fluffy evening dress around me. It is raining. The rain is spoiling my dress. The carriage moves too slowly. We are lost. I want to get back to the castle. I call for a taxi. Buyancy [sic]. Exilaration [sic]. Feet twinkling. I do not mind being wet I'm so happy. (Diary 34, pp. 197-198)

Another evening dress that Nin wrote of in the diary was green, sometimes described as "Oriental green" or "Nile green." The dress appeared to have been especially memorable for Henry Miller, in particular, who thought she looked like a legendary princess when she wore it one evening:

He fell asleep while I dressed up for a formal dinner. Then he came to my _ room and watched me adding the last touches to my dressing. He admired my Oriental green dress. He said I moved about like a princess. (Diary 35, p. 24)

> And Henry was lying on the couch in my bedroom, and I sat next to him one moment, in my green dress, and cuddled him.. (Diary 35, p. 27)

What does he remember most vividly of our moments together? The afternoon he lay in [*sic*] the couch in my bedroom while I finished dressing for a dinner..[two periods] in my deep green Oriental dress, perfuming myself, with that window openning [*sic*] on a Peleas [*sic*] & Melisende [*sic*] background, and he overtaken by a powerful sense of unreality, of living in a fairytale, with a veil between himself and me, the Princess! (Diary 35, p. 92)

[from a letter from Henry Miller to Nin, copied into the diary:]
"God, I want to see you in Louveciennes, see you in that golden light of the window, in your Nile green dress and your face pale, a frozen pallor as of the night of the concert…[ellipse]" (Diary 35, pp. 159-160)

Outerwear: Capes, Coats, and Jackets

Nin's outerwear when noted in the diaries consisted of capes, coats, and jackets. Capes were especially important in the context of her relationship with June Miller. She first wanted June to try on one of her capes, and then offered to make one like it for June:

> I showed her my black cape which she thought beautiful. I made her try it on. ….I told her I wanted to make her a cape like mine. (Diary 32, pp. 158-159)

After June Miller gave Nin her silver and cat's-eye bracelet, and Nin told her she felt the bracelet took the place of June's fingers around her wrist, June replied that she wanted Nin's cape for her own:

> I told her how her bracelet clutched my wrist like her very fingers, held me in barbaric slavery. She wants my cape to wrap around her body. (Diary 32, p. 190)

Later, Nin mailed a cape to June Miller in New York, as recorded in a letter to June transcribed into the diary: "I want you to wear my cape" (Diary 33, p. 89). June Miller later told Dick (1967): "The only thing Anais gave me was a blue stone ring and a shabby cape" (Dick, 1967, p. 162), which shows that June Miller was not impressed by the cape. June Miller was not the only recipient of one of Nin's capes, however. Nin also sent one to her sister-in-law, Ethel Guiler (Diary 33, p. 201). Nin appeared to have hoped that by wearing her things, Ethel would gain a new understanding of Nin:

> My influence on Ethel in N.Y. She not only wore my necklace, but she reawakened herself to new moods: she sat in her room and cried with unknown feelings. She read Lawrence and was moved. She read the "Well of Loneliness" and was not against it. She wore my sandals, my cape, and did not realize me. (Diary 33, p. 201)

Later, in love with Henry Miller, she described herself as "numb with happiness" and felt her cape was like his arm encircling her when they were not together:

> *Engourdie de Bonheur.* When Henry telephones I feel his voice in my veins. I want him to talk, talk into my veins. I have only one love. I want nobody else. I eat Henry, I breathe Henry. Henry is in the sun. My cape is his arm around my waist. (Diary 34, p. 198)

Nin wore a cape to a summer psychoanalysis session with Dr. Allendy:

> I…put on my hat and cape… (Diary 35, pp. 84-85)

Walking at night in Louveciennes with Henry Miller, wearing a black cape added to an overall ambiance, which made her feel like a "Russian actress":

> Night. Walk. Red moon. The Russian actress, pale, black caped… (Diary 35, p. 185)

The velvet cape Nin wore the night of her brother's concert was to appear in dream imagery as well, something she discussed with her psychoanalyst, Dr. Allendy. She dreamed she was at a banquet and felt cold, so she retrieved the cape. Allendy's interpretation of its appearance in Nin's dream is below:

> I am <u>cold</u> (Cold as I am always either from nervousness or weakness) So I go and get the little black velvet cape I wore at the concert. The cape is talismanic. I wore it at the concert when I was admired and found beautiful by Henry. (The motif of clothes is frequent in my dreams. I had a need of externals, of costume, to enhance my confidence, to express myself. I suffered greatly when we were poor and I was badly dressed because this emphasized my sense of inferiority. (Diary 34, pp. 296-297)

Nin also had an old coat, a black coat, a black velvet jacket, and a rose-colored coat:

> …mud on my old coat when I walk through Louveciennes… (Diary 32, p. 113)

> …the little black velvet jacket… (Diary 32, p. 157)

> …old rose coat with Medici collar. (Diary 32, p. 199)

Travelling by train to Switzerland with her small white dog, in late January 1932, she experienced "an amusing incident" (Diary 33, pp. 21-22). Her "black coat and velvet jacket" had both become covered in white dog hair:

> An Italian man who had tried during all the trip to catch my attention, finally in desperation, came up and offered me a brush to brush off Ruby's hair. The offer amused me, and so I laughed. He was immediately encouraged and rushed to get the brush out of his valise. He came to brush me, but I took off my coat and jacket and brushed them conscienciously [*sic*] and imperturbably. After a while I said, returning the brush: Thank you all the same, but I can't use it, it is too soft. He rushed to get a harder one. Again offered to brush me. Again I set to work. When I was through (and his brush full of white hairs) I thanked him. (Diary 33, pp. 21-22)

On an evening out, with her husband, she wore a jacket of some kind:

> They unfastened my jacket. (Diary 33, p. 150)

Visiting Henry Miller, she wore a coat:

> Impulsively, swiftly I came to the bed, sat very near him, put my face very near his _ my coat slipped off... (Diary 33, p. 162)

Hats and Turbans

Hats and turbans were a part of Nin's everyday and evening dress. As she described in a letter to Eduardo Sanchez, copied into her journal, she was looking forward to wearing a new burnt sienna-colored hat to a meeting with her publisher's assistant:

> Friday Mr <u>Lawrence</u> (!) Drake (secretary) and I will correct the first proofs [of her first book]...[ellipse in AN's text] I will wear a new burnt sienna colored hat over one eye. It's your fault. If you had been here I would have cut it off the mock orange bush on which it grew, and worn it for you first. You could have seen the burnt sienna flame shining from afar in the middle of the subway crowd. (Entry dated November 30, 1931, Diary 32, p. 74)

Later, when making a two-column list, in her diary, titled *"Melanges,"* [*sic*] Nin mused on what she saw as two different sides of her self, the "Abstract" and the "Human." Listed in each column were several of Nin's preferences for dress and appearance, including hats. Under "Abstract" she wrote "preference for expensive hats," while under "Human" she wrote "tricks for altering hats" (Diary 33, pp. 23-24). Other hats that Nin wore were noted as being "Russian" or "Byzantine," but were not described in detail.

> I would think myself interesting in a Russian hat! (Diary 35, p. 73)

> We [Nin and Sanchez] sit in the mellow light [in the restaurant Les Vikings]...I wear a real Russian hat... (Diary 33, p. 153)

> The first day I came to see Allendy I wore...a [B]yzantine hat... (Diary 35, p. 70)

Nin also described her different hats in articulating the tension between wanting to look "interesting" and the simpler way she would dress on vacation:

> Do I think myself interesting in a picture hat, soft dress, little make up, as I am in Switzerland? No. But notice what importance I give to externals! I would think myself interesting in a Russian hat! (Diary 35, p. 73)

Turbans were another head covering something Nin wore, both indoors and outdoors. She wore a black turban when she went to meet June Miller one day in January 1932 (Diary 32, p. 199). Dancing with Sanchez one evening, she wore a purple turban:

> In the purple halo of my turban my eyes he [Eduardo] says, shine green and demoniac... (Diary 36, p. 77)

Other Accessories

Nin wore and carried a few other accessories not discussed above, namely gloves, handbags, and handkerchiefs. She mentioned wearing a Spanish *mantilla* with her Spanish dance costume, which is noted in discussion of that costume. Other accessories, such as gloves and handbags were not described in great detail, if they were mentioned at all:

> I see the tiny hole in my glove... (Diary 34, p. 240).

> ...a new handbag, new gloves... (Diary 36, p. 108)

Nin gave one handkerchief to June Miller and at least one to Henry Miller. Her handkerchiefs were usually described as being "wine colored" and the one she gave to Henry Miller was chiffon:

> She had said she wanted nothing from me but the perfume I wore, and my wine colored handkerchief. (Diary 32, p. 160)

> And not knowing what else to say I spread on the bench, between her and me, the wine colored handkerchief she wanted... it was blood I wanted to lay before June's beauty... (Diary 32, pp. 163-164)

He also carries one of my wine colored chiffon handkerchiefs. (Diary 34, p. 265)

Sleepwear and Loungewear

Nin's sleepwear and loungewear received relatively little mention in the diaries.

[at home in Louveciennes:] I lie on the green couch, in my orange kimono. White fur around my neck. (Diary 34, p. 25)

Nin seemed to have preferred to wear pajamas when staying in Henry Miller's apartment, some of which were red silk:

I have left my pyjama[s][*sic*], comb, powder, perfume, in Henry[']s room. (Diary 34, p. 64)

Yet Henry and I were enjoying our togetherness - - undressing, talking, placing our clothes over a chair. Henry was admiring my Japanese red silk pyjamas [*sic*] which looked so strange in the plain room, on the rough blanket...[ellipse in text] (Diary 34, pp. 69-70)

Hugh went to London..[two periods] I met Henry, carrying my pyjama[s] [*sic*] and comb and toothbrush... (Diary 35, p. 55)

Miller had pajamas, too apparently:

We sit in the garden [at the house in Louveciennes], in our pyjamas. (Diary 35, p. 178)

Cosmetic Surgery

Bair (1995) wrote that Nin had cosmetic surgery when she spent the month of February 1932 at a spa in Switzerland, and again in March 1932: "She had mended herself...spending February at a Swiss spa where she had massages, drank the waters, and had the tip of her downward drooping nose surgically removed" (Bair, 1995, p. 132), and "The tip of flesh on her nose was removed in Switzerland in March [1932]…" (Bair, 1995, p.549). According to Nin (1986, p. 41, & Diary 32, 33, & 33 *Bis*), Nin went to Switzerland in late January 1932 and returned in early February, after staying at a shabby pension and a hotel. No mention of the spa experience and surgeries Bair described were found in the sources above, but I did find a vivid description of Nin having cosmetic surgery on her nose in July 1932, a few days before a vacation in Austria. In the diary (Diary 35), Nin described her feelings before, during, and immediately after.

> These days I occupy myself with frivolities…[ellipse] I serve the goddess of beauty, working for her that she may grant me gifts…I'm going to risk on Monday an operation which will forever efface the upward humorous tilt of my nose!
>
> Extremes, perhaps _ _ but I needed this respite from pain and depths. (Diary 35, p. 108)

Nin chose not to tell any of her family, including her husband Hugh, or Henry Miller, in advance of the procedure, and even wrote of how she planned to would "disappear" if the surgery were unsuccessful:

> At half past one Monday Henry left me, thinking I was going to Allendy and then leaving that night. At 2 o'clock I was at the Clinic. And I was amazed at my coming there, all alone, to take a great risk with my face, my life..I lay on the operating table, my heart beating very faintly _ _ aware of every incision and gesture of the Doctors. All at once calm, frightened, courageous. How I planned this hour, letting all the family go – telling nobody – My sense of solitude was immense, and with it a strange <u>sureness</u> which carried me through. I even planned that if the operation failed and my face was marred I would disappear completely _ never see the loved ones again! That moment when I saw my nose in the mirror, blood stained and straight—Greek! Then the bandage, the swelling, the painful night—dreams_
>
> Decision – unfaltering. Why does this come to me only occasionally..[two periods] (Entry dated July 12, 1932, Diary 35, pp. 113-114)

> The nose immense. Lost delicacy. Will the nostril [*sic*] quiver again as they did? (Entry dated July 12, 1932, Diary 35, p. 114)

> Home. Tired out. Haunted by the wonder of the hours with Henry, and by a belated horror of the clinic. My nose is heavy, but beautiful! (Entry dated July 12, 1932, Diary 35, p. 115)

As July 12, 1932 was a Tuesday, and Nin had written of the surgery as being scheduled for a Monday (Diary 35, p. 108), I believe the operation was on Monday, July 11, 1932. Nin had originally made plans to spend the previous Sunday evening with her cousin Eduardo Sanchez, but had Henry Miller at the house with her and chose not to answer the gate when Sanchez arrived as planned and rang the bell (Diary 35, pp. 111-112). After the procedure, she wrote Sanchez a letter on the clinic stationery explaining that she had overdosed on cocaine:

> In the morning the nurse brings me writing paper stamped with the name of the clinic. This suggests an idea—I write to Eduardo in faltering writing—that I have been to the country—taken cocaïne—brought to the hospital because I wouldn't awaken. Why awaken? I had been out of the inferno for 24 hours. I played with the idea—chuckling, as I wrote. To make life more interesting. Yes. (Diary 35, pp. 114-115)

After recovering briefly at home, Nin left on vacation, indicating that her recovery was relatively quick and that the surgery was perhaps not especially drastic:

> House in order. The trunk packed in the entrance. Emilia sewing. Austrian money in my bag. Ticket for Innsbruck. (Diary 35, p. 117)

Later, Nin dreamed of her finding new nose deformed, and then discovering she had only been using a magnifying mirror:

> In the dream my nose was large like a ship funnel. I held it before a mirror and could look up into it as into a funnel. At the bottom there was a mount of small pieces of cotton. The front was a dilated nostril, voracious and palpitating. I marveled at the size and

> investigated. Then I discovered the mirror contained a magnifying glass—that when I turned away my nose was a normal size. (Entry dated July 14, 1932, Diary 35, p. 121)

After traveling to Austria, where she was joined by her husband for their vacation, Nin dreamt that June Miller had come to visit her, and had immediately given her opinion of Nin's "new nose." Naturally, Nin also wondered what Henry Miller would think, and in her dream was worried that June would tell him about it.

> [June] Began to criticize my appearance. When she said my nose was too thick I explained to her about the operation. Then I immediately regretted it because I realized she would tell Henry. (Diary 35, p. 129)

Nin described how she was "touched" by her husband's reaction to the unexpected change and wondered how Henry Miller would react:

> Hugh was distressed by my perfect nose: ["]But I <u>loved</u> that funny little tilt! I don't like to see you <u>change</u>!" Finally I convinced him of the aesthetic progress, but he regrets the typical, characteristic imperfections! That touched me. How one gets to love a being so absolutely that perfection is immaterial _ _ secondary, unnecessary. Wonder what Henry will say! (Diary 35, pp. 133-134)

Henry Miller's reaction to Nin's altered nose was not recorded in the journal, but Nin did describe in detail how she was dressed the first day they saw each other after her vacation in Austria. Perhaps her dramatic makeup was intended to distract from the change, as he did, according to Nin, hardly recognize her when he first saw her standing on the front steps of her home, waiting to greet him. The incident is discussed in findings on Nin's Spanish dance costume, below.

Spanish Dance Costume

> ...punishment of my inordinate love for costume and ornament by giving Elvira my favorite Spanish dress (Diary 32, p. 35)

After her summer vacation with her husband, Nin felt the need to greet Henry Miller with a dramatic scene and stimulate some jealousy on his part. Dressing in what she called her *Maja* costume from her Spanish dancing days, with dramatic makeup, jewelry, and flowers in her hair, she greeted Miller, pretending to have just received a letter containing a marriage proposal from John Erskine (Diary 35, p. 174), who was supposed to have sailed to France on August 12, 1932 (Diary 35, p. 25):

> I wanted to make Henry jealous, but I am too faithful—so I dug into the past & created a legend. (Diary 35, p. 172)

> First—oh, first, I dressed up in my *Maja* costume, flowers, jewelry, make up—hardness, brilliancy. I was angry—full of hatred – I had arrived the night before – we had slept in a hotel _ I thought he had betrayed me – He swears not. It does not matter. I hated him because I loved him as I have never loved anyone. I stand at the entrance when he comes in. Stand. Hands on my hips. Pride and strength. I look out of a burnt, angered, savage self. I stand. Henry comes up dazed and does not recognize me. Does not recognize me_until he comes very near and I smile and speak to him. He cannot believe…[ellipse] The dramatic element of it—the character_Where is the soft self. He thinks I have gone mad. Then before he has quite awakened, I take him to my room. In the fireplace there is a fire [in summer]. There is standing on the grate, the large photograph of John, and his letters [*sic*, plural]. They are burning, burning. I smile. I smile. Henry sits on the couch. "You frighten me, Anaïs—you are strange—different—so dramatic." – I sit on the floor between his knees – I hate you[,] Henry – That story about Jeanne—a half-lie. You lied to me.
>
>   Answers me so gently, that I believe him. And if I do not believe him it doesn't matter. All the treacheries in the world don't matter. I am gay, soft again. John is burnt. The present is magnificent. Only today, only tonight is the apotheosies [*sic*] of all life. Henry asks me to undress. Everything is off, shed, but the black lace mantilla. Henry asks me to keep it, and lies on the bed watching me. I stand before my mirror shedding carnations, ear rings. Henry looks through the lace at my body. (Diary 35, pp. 176-178)

Body Image

> Henry saying: Are you still gaining weight[,] Anaïs?
> Yes _ continuously.
> ["]Oh, Anaïs, don't gain weight,["] says Fred. ["]I like you as you are _ as you are."
> Henry smiles. "But Henry likes Renoiresque bodies!["] I say.
> It's true, says Henry.
> But I love slenderness—I love virginal breasts. [said Fred]
> (Diary 34, p. 196)

Contrary to beauty norms of the early 1930s, Nin expressed numerous times in her diary that she felt inadequate for her small-breasted and slender body type and envied June Miller, whom she saw as curvaceous and attractive. Nin was even concerned that she was potentially undeveloped due to some underlying pathology:

> Talk of physical facts. I am underweight. A few pounds more would give me a security which would greatly add to my assurance. Will he add physical medicine to the psychic treatment? I confess the fear I have had that my breasts are small perhaps because I have masculine elements in my and half my body is therefore adolescent. Allendy begins to question me: are they absolutely undeveloped? No. As we flounder in talk I say: To you the Doctor, I'll simply show them to you." And I do. Then he laughs at my fears. Perfectly feminine small but very outlined breasts—lovely figure. A few pounds more, yes, but how disproportionate my self criticisms! "You are really lovely,["] says Allendy, ["]so much peculiar grace of movement, charm, so much race [*sic*] and finesse of lines." And I begin to laugh. But I ask him to observe what a state this talk has put me into: my hands are cold and moist, my heart is beating, and my face is flushed. He is amazed. No knowledge of my true physical charms can efface the painful doubts of my childhood. (Diary 34, pp. 153-154)

Nin's second concern about her body was that it was too delicate and not strong enough to do all that she wanted to do in life. She often described herself as physically weak. In frustration, she wrote of her ill health as "treacherous," saying that she wished she had more "stamina" (Diary 33, pp. 236-237) This physical weakness was something she also shared with her husband to some degree:

> It is painful for both of us [Nin and Guiler] to admit that we are sub-normal in health and that I shall never realize all the activities I plan for. So far, since my return [from vacation], in spite of ten days of illness I have followed all the plans I made in Mallorca. But occasionally we have to refuse invitations, and they always seem to come too often. (Diary 32, pp. 32-33)

Nin also described her body as fragile and weak:

> It's funny to be so full of abstract, inca[n]descent energy while actually my physique is useless to me, weak, crumbly. I feel sick, so sick, and yet I am blown and tense like Mussolini – I feel dizzy with biliousness as I write, and ecstatic. (Entry dated December 16, 1931, Diary 32, pp. 98-99)

> Confession, to you [the journal] alone, of my <u>physical</u> failure—the treacherousness of my health which always fails me at great moments. Oh, the tragedy of this for me, being more alive and more ambitious than my body can bear! The physical *impuissance*! So many times in my life I have come to the <u>breaking point</u> (after the housework in Richmond Hill, after the dancing, in New York, after June.) The psychological disturbances are all cleared up—there is nothing wrong, except the fragility. Now when I am living the richest period of my life, again it fails me. All the doctors say the same thing: no illness, nothing wrong, but general weakness, low stamina—the heart barely beats, I am cold, I am easily tired out. Today I was <u>tired out</u> for Henry—How precious the moment in the kitchen, with Fred too—while they were eating breakfast at 2 o'clock—" (Diary 33, pp. 236-237)

Further, Nin wrote of both her and Henry Miller's perception of her body as breakable and fragile, especially when compared to that of June Miller, who Nin saw as curvaceous and in possession of a "strange man like strength" (Diary 32, p. 136).

> "You and June wanted to embalm me," I said to Henry.
> Because you seem so utterly fragile. (Diary 33, p. 103)

> Does he make such notes as: Anaïs: —green comb with black hair on it. Indelible rouge. Barbaric necklace. Breakable. Fragile. (Diary 33, p. 130)

> He held me with a kind of fear: "you seem so breakable—I am afraid to kill you." And I did feel small in his bed, naked, with my barbaric jewelry tinkling— small and strong. (Diary 33, pp. 131-132)

> I could feel at once my strength and my fragility, the strength of life so inexorable that the full body of June would triumph royally over all else—our illuminations, understanding, mind…and I would fall tragically because I was woven out of them, and humanly I was fragile… (Diary 33, p .215)

At times, Nin experienced the sense that she had become more like June Miller, in dress, voice, body, and gestures:

> When I talk I feel her in me. I feel my voice heavier, and my face heavier. I am aware of her in me. Facially, I feel altered. A foreign presence. (Diary 32, p. 151)

> The work of art which June is, the painting, the sculpture, the symphony..[two periods] what she incarnates I emanate it. I am the radium which should not rest in her body. I have renounced my body. I inhabit June's body. (Entry dated May 4, 1932, Diary 34, p. 121)

Describing one of her first hotel room encounters with Henry Miller, Nin wrote of paradoxically feeling both small and strong, and compared herself to June Miller's figure, with its "billowing flesh." She ended by giving Henry Miller credit for having, like Pygmalion, sculpted her and made her, a faun, into a woman:

> He held me with a kind of fear: "you seem so breakable—I am afraid to kill you." And I did feel small in his bed, naked, with my barbaric

jewelry tinkling— small and strong. And he felt the strength of the core of me, that core of me which burns at his touch.

Think of that Henry, when you hold my too fragile body in your arms, a body your [*sic*] scarcely feel because you are so used to billowing flesh—but feel the incandescent joy, the movements of its joy like the undulations of a symphony—not the static clay heaviness, but the dancing of it in your arms—fluid—an infiltration—It is a new world: an infiltration. Feel the infiltration of me, not the compact statuary. You will not break me. You are molding me like a sculptor. The faun is to be made woman. (Diary 33, pp. 131-132)

Frailty. Sweet, treacherous acquiescence. Bird docility. You became a woman with me. I was almost terrified by it. You are not just thirty years old—you are a thousand years old. (Diary 35, pp. 201-202)

Notably, in her anticlimactic encounter with John Erskine years earlier, Erskine had said to her, upon seeing her body, that she was a "little faun" (Diary 27, pp. 207-208 & pp. 210-211). Not long after the passage above, however, Henry Miller explained his thinking about her strength and fragility in a letter to Nin that she copied into her journal:

"I don't have a fear that you will want to hurt me. I see that you have a strength too—of a different order, more elusive! No, you won't break. I talked a lot of nonsense—about your frailty." (Diary 33, p. 143)

The Effects of Henry Miller's Appraisal of Nin's Appearance

...his discovery of my buttocks which he finds beautiful— (Diary 33, p 204)

He takes my hands. "For example, your hands, I had never noticed them. Fred gives them so much importance. Let me look at them— Are they really as beautiful at that? Yes—" I laugh.

"You appreciate other things, perhaps." (Diary 33, p. 269)

Nin wrote of several crucial moments in which Henry Miller told her his opinion on whether or not he thought she was beautiful, and they all affected her deeply. In the first incident, when he told her that he disagreed with their friend Alfred "Fred" Perlès, who thought she was beautiful, she was dismayed enough to be moved to tears, and kicked and scratched Miller in response:

> We were reading the red journal [Diary 33]. He came to a phrase Fred had said: that I was beautiful.[14] You see, said Henry, Fred thinks you are beautiful. I don't—I think you have great charm, yes..[two periods]
>
> I was sitting close to him. I looked at him with bewilderment, and then swiftly, my head fell down on the pillow and I cried. When he put his hand on my face he felt the tears. He was amazed. "Oh, Anaïs, I never thought that could mean anything to you_I hate myself for having said that so _ crudely. But you remember, I also told you I didn't think June was beautiful. The most powerful women have not been the most beautiful..[two periods] But to think I could make you cry – that I could do that, when that is one thing I never want to do to you.
>
> He now sat in front of me, and I lay sunk in the pillows, hair rumpled, eyes swimming in tears. At that moment I remembered what the painters thought of me, and I told him. And suddenly I <u>kicked</u> him - - I pawed him, he said, like a cat. And when that was over, which amused him, we [felt][15] strangely closer__until I said in the train, teasingly, because he was telling me he loved to contradict, and that he had thought me beautiful the first day he had seen me, but had begun to think no [*sic*] because Fred insisted so much_ _ And thinking of June too, I said: "You've got bad taste." (Diary 34, pp. 75-77)

---

[14] See Diary 33, p. 245: "'You are beautiful, you are <u>really</u> beautiful," says Fred, eagerly.'

[15] Nin often did not cross her Ts, so this word appeared as "fell" in the diary. In most cases, context made her meaning clear and transcription of her text accounted for this idiosyncrasy in Nin's handwriting; in these case, I believe she intended to write "felt," although "fell" may have been the word she chose.

Despite Henry Miller's explanation and apologies, Nin understandably felt uncomfortable when he wanted to watch her undress before they went to bed that night. She had put on a good face for the remainder of the day, and even considered her hurt to be "an illness," but her comfort in being observed by Miller had suffered:

> But all the wonderful things he had said to me about my journal paled now. My confidence wavered. On the surface I was brave—inwardly, something crumbled. Knowing with my intellect what a relative thing beauty is and that each man has his own individual response—that did not heal me. It is an illness to be so hurt. Yet I took this hurt into myself and I said: ["]I'm going to bear it, I'm going to live it down, I'm not going to care. I don't care." And for a few hours I waved my courage about – until – we were undressing that night and Henry said: I want to watch you undress. I've never done that. And I sat on his bed...[ellipse] and some strange feeling of timidity overcame me. My gestures were shy. I was withdrawn again. I did something to distract his attention from my dressing. I slipped into the bed. I wanted to cry. (Diary 34, pp. 77-78)

Not long after this incident, Nin discussed her "sense of inferiority" in terms of her attractiveness, especially her slenderness, with Dr. Allendy, and reflected on how her various pursuits in life were followed in compensation for the lack she perceived in her appearance:

> I have a sense of inferiority due to first physical weakness. It seemed to me that men only loved healthy and fat women. Eduardo talked to me about fat Cuban girls. Hugh's first attraction was for a fat girl. Everybody used to comment on my slenderness and Mother quoted the Spanish proverb: bones only for the dogs. When I went to Havana I doubted my being able to please because I was thin. This theme continues right down to the moment when Henry hurt me by his admiration of Natasha's body because such a "body seemed rich to him."
>
> In compensation against this I did work out a successful life of accomplishments and talents. But whatever success I do get (in society, posing, dancing, or writing) I quickly overlook—as I

overlook my sure and complete possession of Hugh. (Diary 34, pp. 95-96)

> Allendy was amazed at the <u>extent</u> of my lack of confidence.
> "To an analyst of course, it is very clear even in your appearance.["]
> In my appearance?
> Yes – I saw immediately that you have <u>seductive</u> manners and bearing. Only people who are not sure act <u>seductively</u>.
> We laughed at this.
> I felt softened and easier.
> I told him so. (Diary 34, pp. 125-126)

As her affair with Henry Miller developed in 1932, Nin came to feel more comfortable with her appearance when with him, while at the same time he came to think she was beautiful and to tell her so often. At first, not sure whether her psychoanalytic sessions with Dr. Allendy or her romance with Henry Miller were responsible for her new confidence and "cure," she wrote, "Is it Allendy or Henry who are [*sic*] curing me?" (Diary 34, p. 159).

> "I never thought such a frail little thing could have so much power! Did I ever say you were not beautiful? How could I say it! You're beautiful, beautiful." (Diary 34, p. 160)

> I lose my fear of showing myself naked. He loves <u>me</u>. Nothing matters. We laugh at my gaining weight. He has made me change my hair because he did not like the severe Spanish way – I have thrown it back, high, over my ears—and I feel differently. I feel wind-blown. I look younger. I do not try to be the *femme fatale*! It is useless. He says I look like a magazine cover girl. Nothing hurts me! I feel loved for <u>myself</u>—for my inner self—for every word I write, for my timidities, my sorrows, my struggles, my defects—my frailness—nothing matters. (Diary 34, pp. 160-161)

> When we sit in the kitchen now I stretch like a cat, and my voice is deep, and even the gesture I make to reach for a spoon is charged with the happiness Henry gives me. I am <u>at</u> <u>home</u> <u>in</u> <u>Clichy</u>. Louveciennes is not necessary to me. I have dropped my shell. I only

bring to Louveciennes my tiredness from sleepless nights. But a weariness from fullness [*sic*] instead of emptiness, a joyful weariness. (Diary 34, pp. 171-172)

"I see you <u>all</u> now—I see the face of the child, of the dancer, of the sensual woman. You're beautiful." (Diary 34, p. 188)

Beautiful things he says to me, now. My own kind of loveliness is growing on him. (Diary 35, p. 88)

...the most delicate details. He is roused and excited by the beauty of my hands and feet! He has rediscovered me with Renaud because Renaud was so fervent and so exalted about me—my intelligence, my natural charm, beauty of gestures, the fall of heavy eyelids, the walk, the costume, the hospitality. Henry loves to recall his first impression: my extreme <u>womanliness</u>, the meaningfulness of my smile. (Diary 36, pp. 100-101)

Paradoxically, Nin began to "feel loved for…[her] inner self" (Diary 34, p. 161). At the same time, she felt a growing sense of self-confidence relating to her appearance. She changed her hairstyle at Miller's suggestion, which made her feel differently, and she began to put on weight (something that always had been difficult for her; despite this, Miller still called her "frail") (Diary 34, p. 160).

Nin's Abiding Love of Luxury within A Bourgeois-Bohemian Tension

In the fall of 1931, Nin wrote in her journal that she had quite definitely decided to be a fashion follower, rather than a fashion innovator. She described how she had, three years previously, made great effort to wear what she called "eccentric" clothing. At the time that she wrote this, however, she felt while she had succeeded in being three years ahead of fashion, she did not want to be dressed like "every woman." What had once been eccentric had become commonplace.

> I have anticipated the present day fashions by three years. Three years ago I wore eccentric clothes nobody thought of wearing.

> Today every woman wears eccentric clothes, and I don't like it. So I react back to simplicity. Shall I leap forward again? Sit down and think of something to wear which will be worn in three years from now? I don't think so. It takes time to make an art of dressing. I am not so inclined to give it as much time. I [have] let the fashions catch up to my ideas and I think I will now rest back and let the others dress me. As long as I have gone to the end and peak of one art I am satisfied. (Decoration, Costume, dancing) and then it is time to return to the ultimate and unique work of my life, writing. So I believe pioneering in costume is over for me. I accept to be led. I have other things to do. (Entry dated November 11, 1931, Diary 32, pp. 53-54)

As Nin wrote, her choice was to "react back to simplicity." She recognized her ability to focus on "the art of dressing" and conscientiously create fashions that would be ahead of the trends. She felt she had "gone to the end and peak" of several interests, however (interior design, fashion, and Spanish dance), and once accomplished, at lost interest in each. As she wrote above, writing was her abiding interest and the craft and art to which she wanted to devote her time. This resolution to "let the others dress [her]" did not entirely bear out, however, as Nin still dressed distinctively in the period this study addressed (1931-1932), and felt that she did so on her last day with June Miller, when she felt that others were "mocking" and "hostile" in response.

Whether she was content to follow fashion so she could devote more time and energy to writing, Nin continued to take pleasure in dress after she wrote the above entry. In December 1931, she recognized the contradiction within herself as she wrote how she loved perfume but did not mind mud on her "old" coat, or her large dog's paw marks on her stockings.

> After all, I remain an aesthete in the age of non-aesthetes. I love good smells, cleanliness, health, elegance at the table, everything anti-bourgois [*sic*], therefore anti 1931. Perfume, for instance. What has perfume to say in communistic Russia. Taboo. We who are steering in the direction of a modified communism. What sacrifices I would make for a bottle of perfume. Incredible. I am so sound in other ways. I like simple food. I like inexpensive cigarettes. I abhor butlers, chauffeurs; a maid to dress me; *de luxe* suites on board a ship, all the show of autocratic [*sic*] living—I hate it. I love mud on my old coat

> when I walk through Louveciennes—I don't mind Banco's [their large dog] paw marks on my stockings. Chopping wood and gardening I love. (Entry dated December 26, 1931, Diary 32, pp. 113-114)

Notably, it was while walking in the small town of Louveciennes that Nin "loved" mud on her old coat. She acknowledged herself to have been careless about her appearance when she left in a rush for Switzerland in late January 1932, but would probably have been less likely to have worn an old coat with mud on it, with enjoyment, in Paris. She did not seem to be aware of how this was a contradiction of her "love of…cleanliness" (Diary 32, p. 113).

She wrote that she craved "abject living" in some way, but also found out quickly that it was not really for her (Diary 33, p. 61). Before June Miller had left Paris for New York, Nin had begun to feel as if she were becoming like June:

> When I talk I feel her in me. I feel my voice heavier, and my face heavier. I am aware of her in me. Facially, I feel altered. (Diary 32, p. 151)

After her intense few weeks with June Miller in January 1932, Nin was so emotionally and physically exhausted from what she had described as "The intensity [that was] shattering us both" (Diary 32, p. 177), that she wrote in her journal, "When she left I just wanted to sleep for many days" (Diary 32, p. 203). Instead of doing that, however, having begun to feel "suffocated" and "to tiger-pace the house and to say that [she] had to go away" (entry dated January 25, 1932, Diary 32, p. 217), she abruptly left for Switzerland. As she did so, she felt herself dressing like June Miller, something she acknowledged was not like her "usual self" (Diary 32, p. 218):

> …I made all the preparations—careless ones, unlike my usual self—I didn't care about appearances—clothes, etc. I came away hurriedly…[ellipse in text] (Diary 32, p. 218)

> I had dressed very carelessly, and felt as if I were June. The dress I love best now is an old black velvet dress which is torn at the elbows. June's suit was torn at the elbows. (Diary 33, p. 22)

> I am happiest in my black velvet dress because it is old and has torn at the elbows. [from a letter to June Miller, copied into the diary] (Diary 33, p. 89)

Arriving in Switzerland, Nin even gave staying in a second-rate hotel or pension a try, but lasted only one night before giving up, recognizing that despite her romantic sensibilities, she had certain standards for comforts:

> Absolute luxury is not a necessity to me, but beautiful and good things are. I am not a tramp [i.e., a possessionless vagabond, like the Millers]. I can be occasionally chaste, and stripped of all worldly possessions – but not forever. Henry did observe that what he thought merely beautiful in the house turned out to be at the same time of the strictest necessity. At moments of intense mental activity and writing—I can do without the world, but I know if I had been born on a farm my walls would be painted in coral, and my flower pots green, and my peasant dress would be flowered cretonne, always washed & ironed, and my shoes of red linen – and if I had been born in Byzance [*sic*] I would have been the most Byzantine of all, and I would still prefer the Bridge of Jewelry in Florence to most of its museums, and a beautiful piece of material like Fortuny's means as much to me as a good book. Will that pass? Will it seem strange to me someday that I have walked about the house carrying a Florentine *coffre* [*sic*] with cigarettes rather than an ordinary package of camels [*sic*]? Will it seem strange that my shoes are not shoes, but sandals, mocasins [*sic*], ballet slippers, espadrilles, or Russian boots? That my nails do not look like nails but pearls? That my hair is now blacker than a raven's, my eyelashes more heavily painted than a movie star... (Diary 32, pp. 233-234)

Nin preferred shopping for jewelry to Florence's museums and appreciated Fortuny fabric as much as a good book. She observed this in herself and wondered whether it was an enduring character trait, as she wrote "Will that pass?" (Diary 32, p. 234). Nin quickly came to realize that, as attractive as she found June Miller, June's particular aesthetic was not something she wanted to experience for herself. Nin described how she gave June Miller's "sloppy" living a try, but simply found it unpleasant and unappealing:

> I love her [June Miller], as she is, as she is I worship her. Disorder, chaos, incongruities, mindlessness—my antithesis. In every detail. I have tried wearing careless, sloppy clothes, living in sloppy hotels—I can't do it. The heavy melancholy which always fills me then becomes heavy and suffocating. I had to move from Sonloup because the altitude strained my heart. I came down to Glion on a dismal day, to find all the hotels hugging the railroad track. And second class hotels are so unromantically shabby. (Diary 32, p. 245)

Inspired by the Millers' dramatic and bohemian life, and her reading of Dostoevsky, Nin decided to try a Russian-owned pension that billed itself as a villa instead of one of the hotels along the railroad tracks. Nin lasted only a night:

> Is this the pension Pierre? I asked. "The <u>villa</u> Pierre, she answered. …. It was a big (too big[,] of course) rambly house, sad, smelly. …. I took the room. It was sunny then—I liked the Russian disorder about—cats, dogs, birds, dozens of snow boots and coats and canes. … I laid Dostoevsky on the night table. And I knew all the while that I was being romantic, that I probably would be uncomfortable and it would not be good for me….Dinner was late - - and it was very bad. …. the next day I had to eat with them and the Princess had come in my room and sat down – and an hour after our meal together I was settled in an ordinary hotel, where the impersonality and impeccable cleanliness and food that did not smell of cabbage soothed my miserable mood. I had run away from the romantic. I wanted a rest from the romantic. I liked having my dinner on time! I looked around at the neatness of my dress and room and decided I was at least not as romantic as June. (Diary 32, pp. 245-248)

Sitting in her hotel room, probably feeling the effects of being at a higher altitude than Paris, Nin appears to have become intoxicated on "two fingers of 'Malaga doré' [a liqueur]" (entry dated, February 3, 1932, Diary 33, p. 8). She wrote that she had felt she needed "a tonic," but found instead it made "the room heave," gave her a sense of "stupid beatitude," and gave her a headache, after which she then began to take stock in her shoes, toiletries, and the hemline of her old coat (entry dated, February 3, 1932, Diary 33, pp. 8-9).

> I observe my boots, my mocasins [*sic*] and my dressy shoes lined up regimentally in a corner of the room; my bottles lined up with exquisite symetry [*sic*]; my books close set and tidy. My desk tidy. My green comb broke in two. I keep half of it for Ruby's white hair, and half for my black hair, side by side. And only a minute or so ago I stood before the mirror and said irritably: ["]If I must wear an oldish and shabbish black coat, there is no reason in the world why it shouldn't hang just right. I must fix that hemline. (Entry dated February 3, 1932, Diary 33, pp. 9-10)

Tseëlon wrote that "Dressing well is bound up with self-esteem and feeling good *even* on one's own" [emphasis in the original] (Tseëlon, 1997, p. 63), and this is evident in Nin's thoughts, recorded alone in her hotel room in Switzerland. Nin had given June Miller's sloppy, shabby carelessness a try, but it was not a state that she was truly comfortable with, as evidenced by Nin's preference for tidiness and order, and her discomfort with disorder. After all, Nin saw herself as very different from June Miller. In her own estimation, Nin, by contrast, was ethical, responsible, scrupulous, proud, and bourgeois:

> What did it matter all I thought the day before. She was un-ethical [*sic*], irresponsible – it was her nature. I would not tamper with her nature. My pride about money matters was bourgois [*sic*]. I was less fantastic in the same proportion as I was scrupulous and proud. (Entry dated January 20, 1932, Diary 32, p. 198)

Interestingly, she described her love of beauty, colors, perfumes, as an almost exclusively feminine trait, except for poets, like Hugh:

> In that world of intricate voluptuousness women live <u>alone</u>– except for the poets. Hugh is the poet who lives in that world—*la volupté des couleurs, des parfums, des étoffes—il la connait* [*sic*], *lui*.[16] (Diary 32, p. 235)

---

[16] Translation: "The voluptuousness of colors, perfumes, and stuffs [i.e., fabrics]—he knows it."

As much as she rejected June Miller's bohemian living, Nin still betrayed a fascination with it. She not only copied into her diary Henry Miller's collected notes he had made on his wife in preparation for his autobiographical novels. She also recorded some of the fantastic stories June Miller had told her as well. The excerpted story below includes a mention of a Romanian shirt, a typical Greenwich Village bohemians' Eastern European-inspired style (Saville, 2003):

> The policeman was worried, and stared at her pale face. "Where do you live?" She got angry and offered to show him where she lived, if he wished, and has he did wish it, she took the cop to their hotel room where Henry was still lying in bed in a Roumanian [*sic*] embroidered shirt. The table was covered high with manuscripts and books, and he could see they were intellectuals, bohemians, anyway. (Diary 32, pp. 249-250)

As she reflected on June Miller's personality in the diary, Nin appeared to have done some self-analysis, as well. In a two-column list of what traits she attributed to the two sides of her own nature, the "Abstract" versus the "Human," Nin included some of her preferences for dress and living (Diary 33, pp. 23-24): Her abstract side had "love of…stylized decorations; artificiality in details; elaborate Byzantine costume" and "aristocracy of manner." In contrast, the corresponding qualities on her human side were "love…wild Scotch gardens; of log fire[s] in fireplaces; of plain costumes; [and] love of naturalism in others" (Diary 33, p. 23). Further, whereas her aristocratic, abstract side had an "understanding of [the] poor" and "sympathy for them," her human side felt a "dislike of poor's proximity, disgust at their dirt, smell" (Diary 33, p. 23). In a list of things Nin's mother actively disliked ("Mother's Prejudices"), Nin included the following: Bohemians, "dyed hair," and make-up (Diary 33, p. 37), suggesting that Nin socialized with people who might fit the bohemian stereotype (or at least, that she had an interest in doing so). Hugh, on the other hand, while perhaps not "prejudiced" against them, instead "endured" them and acted as an artists' patron:

> [Hugh] Endures my friendships with low class people, bohemians, *sans-le sous* [*sic*] – characterless, conscienceless.
> Gives them money. (Diary 33, p. 38)

Examining issues of social class, the Guilers and the Nins both saw themselves as upper-middle class. The Nin family had fallen somewhat after the separation of Nin's mother and father, which made Nin herself very conscious of being badly dressed when living in New York as a child. Before her parents' separation, the family had received support from Rosa Culmell Nin's father, the Danish Consul to Havana and the owner of a prosperous imports business. After the death of Nin's maternal grandfather, Joaquín Nin y Castellanos had left his wife for a young heiress.

Hugh Guiler, by contrast, had been born in Boston, raised in Puerto Rico, and educated at boarding school in Scotland, followed by a college education at Columbia University in New York. His family were protestant and after he graduated from Columbia University he went into banking. According to Guiler, he and his wife were from an entirely different social class than the Millers. As he wrote in his journal, the Guilers were aristocrats, whereas the Millers were "peasants":

> ...I know that what Anaïs enjoys, what stimulates her in Henry's admiration is the very fact that he is not her type, as I am. Anaïs and I are aristocrats. Henry is, as I believe he himself has said, the peasant and it is an instinct seeking balance that makes her seek his company, that stimulates her imagination. There could be no greater contrast than between these two. One has gone to the extreme of dirt and degradation; for all my admiration for his genius his writing has given me the physical sensation of a bad odor that I cannot rid my imagination of. The other is all that is the most refined, at times in the past even to the point of decadence. The desire of both for balance is a natural one. But as always it is Anaïs who has proved herself the stronger. While absorbing through her imagination whatever the peasant had to give her and becoming stronger by it, it is she who has come out the leader as aristocrats always have who, like the French, have the instinctive wisdom to renew their strength in the earth. (Entry dated March 8, 1932, Journal of Hugh P. Guiler, pp. 81-83)

When Nin met Henry Miller, he was admittedly fascinated with grittier details of his own down-and-out experience, living in Paris, which were to become his autobiographical novel, *Tropic of Cancer* (Miller, 1934/1961). Nin took note of those things, writing:

> *Il a des gouts* [*sic*] *crapuleux, bourgois*[17] [*sic*]. He likes the smell of urine, cabbage[,] etc. Refinement bothers him. He loves curses, and slang, prostitutes—dumps, apache quarters, squalor, toughness. (Diary 33, p. 35)

Despite such differences in their tastes, Nin came to find Henry Miller attractive. Not long into their affair, she was so in love with him that she found she could, unexpectedly, withstand the "flat visual attack" of ugly things such as the sight of his khaki shirt, hanging on a peg in his hotel room (Diary 33, p. 138):

> I am impervious to the flat visual attack of things. I see your khaki shirt hung up on a peg. It is your shirt and I could see you in it..[two periods] you wearing a color I detest. (Diary 33, p. 138)

> It is his khaki shirt, and he is the man who is the axis of my world now. I revolve around his richness of being… (Diary 33, p. 139)

The Guilers and Nin's mother were not the only ones acutely aware of the class difference between Nin and the Millers. Henry Miller commented on it as well, observing that she was an "aristocrat" at heart, and could never really change her social class:

> He observes above all, my aristocracy. From that first phrase: it was presumptious [*sic*] of me - - I am the peasant - -
> I sit on his bed, with my wide rose dress spread around me, smoking, and he observes the spectacle. He tells me he will never take me into his life, to the places he has told me about—that for me all the trappings and surroundings are right and fitting—that I must have them. "You couldn't live otherwise." I contemplate his sordid room and I exclaim: I think it is true. If you put me in this room, and poor, I would start all over again _ _
> I tell him about salons, and titles, and coats of arms, and I bring all that into his room. And he marvels. (Diary 33, pp. 124-125)

---

[17] Translation: "He has villainous, bourgeois tastes."

It was the tension between the Guilers' class position and Nin's interest in the Millers that was one of the primary findings in this study. Nin wanted to experience a wide range of experiences in life to help her have more real-world experience to inform her writing practice. She was fascinated by June Miller and her rough, bohemian life, and tried to emulate it to some degree, but found it was not to be a lasting transformation. She had a passing interest in becoming like June Miller, dressing like her, and looking like her, as demonstrated above. In reality, however, in her dress Nin remained, as her husband wrote above, "all that is the most refined" (Journal of Hugh P. Guiler, p. 82).

Chapter 5
Discussion and Conclusions

Overview

This chapter presents analysis and synthesis of findings, discusses relevant theory and literature to support conclusions, addresses limitations and makes suggestions for future research. The discussion of key research findings and Tseëlon's (1997) Third Paradox, the Visibility Paradox, is summarized below. Also included in this chapter are the conclusions, implications, and suggestions for future research studies.

"Beautiful and good things"

> I might be thrown into the slumps a hundred times and each time I would clamber out again to good coffee, on lacquered trays, by the side of an open fire. Each time I would clamber out to silk stockings and perfume. Absolute luxury is not a necessity to me, but beautiful and good things are. I am not a tramp. I can be occasionally chaste, and stripped of all worldly possessions – but not forever. (Diary 32, pp. 232-233)

This study discovered the dress and appearance of Anaïs Nin in a crucial period in her life, as expressed in her diaries from October 1931 through

October 1932. The results uncovered Nin's writings on her dress practices, body image and self-confidence, and brought new information to light. For example, the triangulation of data found in the diary of Hugh Guiler corroborated Nin's diary descriptions of her "nacreous" nail polish. The discovery of discrepancies between Bair (1995) and Nin (1986, and Diaries 32-36) established a rationale for the rejection of Bair's descriptions of Nin's dress practices in 1931-1932 (1995). Building on Boucheraud (2012), this study established an accurate timeline of events regarding the creation of Nin's second Diary 33, Diary 33 *Bis*, and her cosmetic surgery and other dress practices in July 1932. In this study, I read, transcribed, and analyzed the diaries for every detail of Nin's dress practices and appearance in October 1931 – October 1932 were described in detail. As other scholars have noted, Anaïs Nin was attracted to June Miller. This study discovered how brief Nin's interest in emulating June Miller's way of dress and lifestyle had been. Further findings included Nin's examination of her dress practices in the context of psychoanalysis. The influence of her affair with Henry Miller on her hairstyle, dress, body image, and self-esteem were established. Additionally, the data on Nin's brief, and reluctant, affair with her cousin Eduardo revealed how she used the symbolism of shopping for jewelry, perfume, and cosmetics, and the purchase of two steel bracelets, as a means for liberation from his desire for her. This study's findings on Nin's descriptions of her dress and dress practices revealed that Nin had an abiding love of "beautiful and good things" (Diary 32, p. 233), felt her self-esteem enhanced by Henry Miller's admiration of her appearance, and had a keen awareness of her appearance and its effects on herself and others. Nin enjoyed physical comforts and beautiful clothing. She was aware of Henry Miller's fascination with slum living and her own fascination with June Miller's bohemian ways. Although Nin spent many days and nights in Henry Miller's apartment in Paris, she was never to give up her bourgeois life with her husband Hugh Guiler (not even after her bigamous 1955 marriage to Rupert Pole). She may have sacrificed on her dress in some respects, by wearing mended stockings to save to be able to spend money on gifts for Henry Miller, but she also made cosmetic surgery a priority. As Nin herself wrote, "Absolute luxury is not a necessity to me, but beautiful and good things are" (Diary 32, pp. 232-233). As this study found, for Nin, those "beautiful and good things" included French perfumes and silk stockings. Nin's interest in Russian fashions was likely linked to the Russian émigré community and their presence in Paris's fashion industry (Vassiliev, 1998; Vaughan, 2006). These dress practices place Nin squarely in the context of life in 1930s Paris. As Tortora & Marcketti (2015) noted, the 1930s was a time for financial restraint in fashion spending, even in Paris. Nin represents an example of an upper-middle class woman who did not have to work for a living, received a monthly allowance from her husband, and was able to spend her discretionary funds on jewelry, perfume, and clothing.

Tseëlon's Paradox Three: The Visibility Paradox

The primary finding of this study was the ways in which Nin's diaries reflected the concepts within Tseëlon's (1997) Third Paradox. Called the Visibility Paradox, this paradox conceived of women as embodying a visual spectacle and yet also socially invisible. In Tseëlon's (1997) conception, the function of women's beauty practices is to render women psychologically invisible, thereby reducing feelings of threat and vulnerability. Nin's diaries contained many descriptions of occasions when Nin felt attractive in social situations, along with descriptions of occasions on which Nin felt uneasy or even threatened because of her appearance. Presented among the findings in Chapter Four were Nin's writings on her body image, her self-esteem, and the impact of Henry Miller's admiration (or lack thereof) of her appearance. Those findings supported Tseëlon's Third Paradox, with its emphasis on women's dress and appearance practices as related to the self made visible. Tseëlon (1997) explained how in familiar and comfortable environments, in the presence of others whose opinions are unimportant, a woman will feel psychologically comfortable and at ease, as she feels that her appearance will not affect others' perceptions of her, resulting in psychological invisibility (Tseëlon, 1997, p. 55). Psychological visibility, on the other hand, is the opposite:

> In an insecure environment one is on display, on show, being examined, and measured. One is invaded by scrutinizing looks, attention or comments; overshadowed by other people's better presentation, or judgement. It is a feeling of being threatened and psychologically *visible*. (Tseëlon, 1997, p. 55, emphasis in the original]

A striking example of this experience, psychological visibility, appeared in Nin's journal, when she had dressed especially for June Miller, and was uncomfortably aware of other people's reactions to her appearance:

> I had dressed ritually for her, in the very costume which created a void between me and other people – a costume which was a symbol of my individualism and which she alone would understand. Black turban, old rose dress with black laced bodice, and black lace collar, old rose coat with Medici collar. I had created a sensation as I walked, and I was lonelier than ever, because the sensation was partly hostile, mocking, flattering, but not comprehensive. (Diary 32, p. 199)

The "sensation" Nin described making, above, was only partly "flattering," for the most part a negative experience. The result was her feeling "invaded by scrutinizing looks" (Tseëlon, 1997, p. 55). Tseëlon (1997) described this kind of awareness as consciousness, which is an awareness of "being the object of the gaze of the Other" (Tseëlon, 1997, p. 55). Tseëlon further defined consciousness:

> Women care about their appearance when there are important things at stake, when being judged or when feeling unsure and anxious. They make effort with their appearance in the company of people they want to impress, in important situations (that require, for example, dressing up), or when there is a formal expectation (for example, work). But they are made conscious of their appearance when something goes wrong (if they are overdressed, underdressed, or inappropriately dressed), or when somebody comments on their appearance (compliment or criticism). (Tseëlon, 1997, p. 55)

The concept of the gaze of the Other comes from the existential philosopher Jean-Paul Sartre and was further articulated by Michel Foucault (1977/1995) in his concepts of discipline and punishment, wherein the individual internalizes the gaze of the other, or society at large. Foucault (1977/1995) used the metaphor of the panopticon, a circular prison in which the prisoners can be observed by guards at all times, knowing they are being observed without knowing precisely when they are being observed, to illustrate the individual's self-policing, or self-discipline, in maintaining social norms. Feminist scholars have applied Foucault's (1977/1995 & 1978/1990) theories to their work, including the discourse surrounding the female body and women's lived experiences in the body (Bartky, 1988; Bordo, 2003; Diamond & Quinby, 1988). Less commonly, scholars of dress have taken this feminist critical approach, and applied Foucault's concepts of discipline and punishment to dress theory (Tseëlon & Kaiser, 1992; Tyner & Ogle, 2009), and those findings support's Tseëlon's (1997) overall framework.

Tseëlon (1997) also referenced the work of Ervin Goffman (1959) in her articulation of Paradox Three, as the paradox addresses how individuals attempt to control others' perceptions of them (impression management) in different social situations. In Goffman (1959), individuals act out social roles by means of various "performances" in everyday life, and others respond to those performance with culturally expected, scripted, performances of their own. Additionally, Goffman theorized that the performer may at times be "fully taken in by his own act," and at other times be quite aware that his performance or "impression of reality" is not actual reality and is only a performance (Goffman, 1959, p. 17). Citing Sartre, Goffman pointed out that in some cases the effort of the performance can result in the performance being the only act accomplished during the performance:

> The attentive pupil who wishes to *be* attentive, his eyes riveted on the teacher, his ears open wide, so exhausts himself in playing the attentive role that he ends up by no longer hearing anything. (Sartre, as cited in Goffman, 1959, p. 33) [emphasis in Goffman]

The effort expended to *appear* attentive therefore takes up all the student's time in the moment and the result is that the student was too busy performing attentiveness to actually absorb the material being presented in class. Dress and feminist scholars have applied Goffman's theories to dress and appearance (Jacob & Cerny, 2004; Moon & Ogle, 2013; Mun, Janigo, & Johnson, 2012). In Nin's experience, she described her psychoanalyst, Dr. Allendy, cautioning her against being taken in by her own performances:

> There was nothing wrong with acting roles except that one must not take them seriously—I become sincere and I go all the way. (Diary 35, p. 72)

As a child of a single mother, Nin often received hand-me-downs from her Cuban cousins, and her mother was sometimes given money by her more well-to-do sisters. Being unable to dress exactly as she liked, under financial constraints, made Nin conscious of her appearance in a way that was at times a source of frustration. By 1931, Nin enjoyed the freedom and disposable income her upper-middle class lifestyle gave her. Having a home in Paris and then its suburb, Louveciennes, meant that the Guiler-Nin household (which, until late 1932 included Nin's mother, Rosa Culmell Nin, and Nin's younger brother, Joaquín Nin-Culmell) often had to host visiting relatives when they came to Europe on vacation. Rosa was the eldest of five sisters and the extended family included many Cuban, American, and Danish cousins who often came to visit the Guiler-Nin family, to see Paris, and shop. Rosa Culmell Nin had, unfortunately, not married well when she married Joaquín Nin, and as a result the couple received support from her father (a wealthy man with a Danish imports business, and the Danish Consul in Havana) until his death. Not long after Rosa's money ran out, her husband left her for a younger, wealthier woman. Rosa received some support from her younger sisters, who *had* married financially well-off men, but Anaïs never felt as well-dressed or financially comfortable as her cousins. The following quote illustrates how, even as an adult, Nin still felt unpleasantly conscious of her appearance when in the presence of her mother's family:

> Seeing my rich aunt Anaïs again always brings back distressing memories of my over-sensitive childhood, when they criticized at the same time as they gave Mother money, when they looked without sympathy on Joaquin's piano playing, my writing, my delicate health, my shyness. I still suffer from malaise before them because as a child I reacted passively, gently, resignedly. Only lately my individuality is stronger and I revolt against any tyranny, and am indifferent to their lack of understanding. However I need all the trappings of my new life, Hugh, my home, my clothes, our car, to make me feel secure, to annihilate the painful memories of dependence, debts, the forced gratitude etc. (Diary 32, pp. 65-66)

Although Nin was able to articulate that she no longer cared what her wealthy relatives thought of her appearance, she also acknowledged that she needed "all the trappings" of her present lifestyle in order "to feel secure" and "annihilate" those "painful memories" from childhood.

Nin continued to envy June Miller's body type, however, having long viewed her own body as frail, weak, and too thin. Tseëlon included the connection between women's "body image and self-concept" in Paradox Three, which makes discussion of Nin's body cathexis and dissatisfaction with her figure type relevant here (Tseëlon, 1997, p. 63). Nin's envy of June's figure and dissatisfaction with her own were often topics she reflected on in her journals and a subject she discussed with her psychoanalyst, Dr. Allendy. Tseëlon wrote "Good appearance is a shield which is easily pierced" (Tseëlon, 1997, p. 63), while Nin described herself as struggling with self-confidence and having a "shell" around her to protect her from others (Diary 34, p. 123). In addition to having this "shell" about her, Nin also described feeling layers of sensation shielding her from others, effectively protecting her from psychological vulnerability, as noted in her description of her experience at her brother's concert (presented in Chapter Four).

Nin's continued consciousness of her appearance in the context of the Visibility Paradox appeared further in her descriptions of her psychoanalytic sessions with Dr. Allendy. When Allendy asked her what her greatest fear was, she replied that it was not being loved on account of her body and described how she envied June Miller's appearance:

> AL. ["]After all, what is the <u>worst</u> of your fears—tell me about them. Let us look at them frankly."
> AN. Merely the realization, or doubt that my absence of health and physical developement [sic], fullness [sic], makes me less loved than I want to be.
> (At the same time I know it is this fear which has incited and developed the <u>artist</u>. I am only unhappy as a woman. And even more so since I have known June who has everything that I do not have: the sensual voice, the physical richness, the abnormal vigor and endurance.)
> AL.[Allendy] Do you realize how many women envy you your silhouette?
> (This kind of assurances [sic] I have often received. It is not the kind which heals; or I would be healed. I know he must find a more profound way of communicating confidence to me – Now he is talking as men talk to me.) (Diary 34, pp. 123-125)

Dr. Allendy also analyzed Nin's dream of attending a banquet and wearing the cape she wore at her brother's concert, explaining the frequent recurrence of clothing in her dreams as signifying her sense of inferiority stemming from lack of appropriate clothing as a child:

> [Allendy's interpretation of her dream of a banquet]: "I am <u>cold</u> (Cold as I am always either from nervousness or weakness) So I go and get the little black velvet cape I wore at the concert. The cape is talismanic. I wore it at the concert when I was admired and found beautiful by Henry. (The motif of clothes is frequent in my dreams. I had a need of externals, of costume, to enhance my confidence, to express myself. I suffered greatly when we were poor and I was badly dressed because this emphasized my sense of inferiority. (Diary 34, pp. 296-297)

One of the notable effects of Nin's affair with Henry Miller was her growing comfort with her appearance when she was with him. Rather than feeling a sense of psychological visibility that led to discomfort and feelings of vulnerability in the early days of their affair, Nin exuded a sense of naturalness (psychological invisibility) that caused Miller to comment on it. That she should feel this naturalness that Miller observed in her, one he noted he himself did not feel ("yet") was in fact "surprising" to her, enough that she marveled at it:

> And I am thinking of his capacity to be awed, which means to sense divinity. When I have been most natural, most womanly, rising out of the bed to get him a cigarette, to serve him champagne, to comb my hair, to dress, he still says: I do not feel natural with you yet. (Diary 33, p. 128)

> I did unexpected things_ surprising to myself. That moment Henry mentions when I sat on the edge of the bed. I had been standing before the mirror combing my hair. He lay in bed and said: I do not feel at ease with you yet. Impulsively, swiftly I came to the bed, sat very near him, put my face very near his _ my coat slipped off, and the straps of my chemise too – and in the whole gesture, in what I said, there was something so feminine, so strangely, so naturally giving, pliant, human – that he couldn't talk. I do that, and afterwards with my analytical mind I dissect it, marvelling [*sic*] at its naturalness– (Diary 33, pp. 161-162)

Later in 1932, Nin described shopping and going to the hairdresser as means to enhance her self-esteem:

> How do I run away from my own moods—and where? The cave of rock crystal, the pure delight of sensual beauty in silk velvet, furs, perfumes, colors, glassware, I wander through the shops as through wonder..[two periods] (Entry dated "September," Diary 36, p. 129)

> So many crutches. The beauty of my house, the intricate loveliness of my costumes_all crutches. Extravagance. I went through a day once when the love of Eduardo, Hugh, Allendy and Henry were all manifested, when the hairdresser saved all the bits of perfume in the bottles to pour over my hair as a gift, when the man who gave samples on the street corner gave me two instead of one, when the Russian taxi driver doffed his cap to me and opened the door of his taxi, when a shop girl caressed my foot while trying on bedroom slippers because she thought it so lovely..[two periods] (Diary 36, pp. 150-151)

Nin also described her beauty as only an "enchantment" (Diary 33, p. 164), writing of herself as fragile in reality, but appearing beautiful only "at certain moments" (Diary 35, p. 27):

> *Je suis belle par les choses crée [sic] par moi dont je suis enveloper [sic].*[18] I am beautiful by the creations of my mind, of my imagination, of my taste – it is all art – Actually, realistically I am a fragile moth-like woman – all the rest is enchantment, wonder, art, art, art! (Diary, 33, p. 164)

> Last night, coming home, I was singing in the car, oh, singing. And at the banquet I <u>ate</u>, things didn't stick in my throat, and I dazzled my partner with warm talk, and I dazzled the host, and the Egyptian Consul, whose dark eyes followed me all evening. My happiness made me natural. I glowed. I was [remembering] lying on the grass with Henry over me, and I was beaming at the poor ordinary people around the table…[ellipse] And they <u>all</u> felt something. They were all

---

[18] Roughly translated: "I am made beautiful by the things I create because they envelop me."

> under my enchantment. Even the women who wondered…[ellipse] who wanted to ask me from what <u>shop</u> I had bought whatever I wore. my face..[two periods] Women always want to know the name and address of the shop. They think when they have my shoes, my hairdresser[,] my face make up, that it will all work the same way. They do not conceive of magic, witchcraft, *ensorcellement* [*sic*]. They don't know that I am not beautiful but that I can appear to be at certain moments..[two periods] more beautiful than really beautiful women! (Diary 35, pp. 26-27)

Nin puzzled over the connection between her dress, appearance, and self-confidence, even discussing the topic with her psychoanalyst, Dr. Rene Allendy, and recording their conversations in her journals. In Nin's experience, she was searching to understand June, but more important overall was her ongoing search for self-understanding. Her journal keeping practice had served that function for many years, but her conversations with Allendy gave her new insights. After meeting Henry Miller in December 1931, but before meeting his wife June Miller, Nin expressed a frustration with herself, based on her falsification of her "true self" and inability to be her "fundamental" self:

> What does it matter what Miller thinks of me? He'll know soon enough exactly how I am. He has a caricatural mind—I'll see myself in caricature. If it is true it doesn't matter. I love ideas. But why do I falsify my true self through the incapacity to express myself in talk? What sort of a crazy personality do I have which does not express the fundamental me? And anyway, why should I care if I don't express myself. And I do care, horribly, when it is a question of Hugh, John, Eduardo, or Miller. I do care. (Diary 32, p. 111)

Contradicting herself in the above passage, Nin expressed first that she thought she should not care what Henry Miller thought of her, then that she *did* care. This frustration and inability to express her "true self" with others, in speech and in dress and appearance, is a topic that recurred in the diary throughout 1932 and a subject she discussed with her psychoanalyst, Dr. Allendy. Nin recounted how she had dressed dramatically for her first session with Allendy, intending to intimidate him after describing how they had analyzed a dream of hers in which she appeared to be an invulnerable, jeweled idol. Allendy interpreted her dream as an expression of what she wished:

> I stood in dark space, dressed luxuriously in brocades and jewels, like a Byzantine idol. I wore a tiara of precious stones. I stood like an idol. People said: "She is a resplendent idol but not a human being." (Diary 35, p. 69)

> …Allendy said the dream did not represent a fear but a <u>wish</u>. I wished to be an idol. What was the characteristic of an idol? Invulnerability. As an idol I intimidated or ruled over people. I preserved myself from pain. It was to conceal my softness, and my purity and my simplicity. It was a mask. Aggressively dazzling in self-protection. The first day I came to see Allendy I wore a draped costume and a byzantine [sic] hat, and I succeeded in intimidating him by my strangeness. The Antinea [sic] of the Atlantis. A desire to be more interesting, more accentuated. A role. I played the role of a sophistication which was not truly my own. (Diary 35, p. 70)

In this case, Nin's clothing was something she used as "armor," for self-protection. Nin's need to dress in a particular way feel to at ease when in Montparnasse with Henry Miller was another example of how she dressed for psychological invisibility:

> In all this he seemed so right. I began to see how much of an <u>armour</u> my costumes had been. I remembered that to please Henry I wear for him softer and more youthful things, and that I hated when he decided to take me to Montparnasse to meet people in <u>these</u> puerile clothes. I wanted so much my draperies and Russian hat. Like an armour! (Diary 35, pp. 70-71)

Allendy's main goal appeared to have been to help Nin to discover her "true self," thereby enabling her to drop all role-playing. According to the diaries, Allendy seemed to have been of the opinion that to be "entirely natural" was the most desirable outcome for Nin. As she wrote in the diaries, he explained this as "reconciling her to her own image," which meant finding her true self and behaving naturally, rather than acting a role:

> I expect someday to be able to <u>reconcile you to your own</u> image (*vous reconsilier [sic] a [sic] votre propre image*)[19]... (Diary 34, p. 281)

> Yes, and until you can act perfectly naturally, according to your own nature you will never be happy. (Diary 34, pp. 288-289)

> Now you see that the more you act like yourself, the nearer you come to a fulfilment [sic] of your real needs....I do not despair yet of reconciling you to your own image. (Diary 34, p. 290)

> He [Allendy] talks about my true rhythm. Finding my true rhythm. (Diary 35, p. 69)

When Nin asked Allendy what this lost true rhythm of hers was, his reply was qualified by first saying it was "too direct a question to answer in psychoanalysis," but that he would try, and give her an answer "in parenthesis" (Diary 35, p. 71):

> As far as he could see, from studying me, I was fundamentally an exotic, Cuban woman, with charm and simplicity and purity—very feminine and soft. <u>All the rest</u> was literary, intellectual, imaginative. (Diary 35, p. 71)

The implication in Allendy's assessment above was that Nin had only one nature and anything else she did was "put on," inspired by literature or her imagination. His comment about her being exotic and Cuban was notable in that Nin had earlier described using her ethnicity as something she could "hide behind":

> I hide behind my foreigness[sic]: it is my shield. Whatever is strange, disconcerting, unusual about me, I let people attribute to the Spanish, or the French, whereas a complete familiarity with any of the nationalities I derive from would prove that I cannot be explained or painted by any one of them—perhaps by all of them, and even then, there would still be strangenesses. (Diary 33, p. 202)

---

[19] Translation: "reconcile yourself to your own image."

Over the course of her sessions with Dr. Allendy, Nin came to see herself as dressing with less attempt to distinguish herself, wearing simpler and more conventional clothing. She was still very aware of how her dress and appearance could give her greater self-confidence when she felt she was lacking it from within. At the same time, she felt that she had developed a greater sense of self worth. Of course, recognizing how her lack of confidence had inspired her creativity, she wondered what would happen to her dress and other creative works if she were to be "cured" by psychoanalysis:

> One of the things he observed was that I was dressing more simply. I have felt much less the need of original costume. I could almost wear an ordinary tailor[ed] suit now. Why? Costume for me has been a very significant exteriorization. Not being certain of my beauty or strength I have designed original, striking clothes which distinguish me from other women. I have compensated with an external expression for the secret lack of self confidence. Having a sense of my own value I can wear a tailor[ed] suit without feeling effaced. When I do not have it, costume helps me, adds to my firm carriage, augments my poise. I suffered so keenly during my girlhood from being badly dressed, which added so much to my sense of inferiority. Now I rely on clothes.
>
> But, I added laughing, now if I get happy and banal, the <u>art of</u> costuming which owes its existence then purely to a sense of insufficiency, will be mortally affected—may even disappear. *La Fecondité de l'Insuffisance.* The pathological basic of creation! What will become of the creator when I get normal?
>
> I don't want to get <u>normal</u>. I will merely gain in strength, so as to live out my instincts more fully—so as to enjoy life more, and be able to experience more. I will develop different & more interesting illnesses. (Diary 34, pp. 301-302)

Preferring to become stronger, rather than more "normal," by late August 1932, Nin had managed to reconcile herself to her true nature, just not in the way that Allendy had intended. She perceived of herself as a woman who played various roles and had many faces, and wrote that she became, paradoxically, authentic and sincere by playing those roles:

> Must tell Allendy that I feel now a continuous sincerity even when I am the fatalistic *sombre* sensual woman—it is no longer a role it has developed from my maturity. I am now those stronger roles I acted before. But I reached them as a natural developement [*sic*], not by mental will. Because they grew and are not acquired, they are real. Because they are real I am not strained and uneasy. I enjoy the variegated moods. I am a woman with a hundred faces. (Entry dated August 28, 1932, Diary 36, pp. 26-27)

Allendy may have described Nin as inherently a woman with "charm and simplicity and purity," but Nin did not want to be confined by this description (Diary 35, p. 71). Like any modern woman, she wanted to exercise agency in determining who she was. Wambly Bald had written of June Miller, saying "It is evident that June is one of those modern women who choose to ride their impulses" (Bald, 1987, p. 88). Before meeting June Miller and clipping Bald's article on her and inserting it into her journal (Diary 32), Nin already showed signs of having resolved that this living by impulse was the path that she had chosen. She was certainly intrigued and inspired by June and Henry Miller and their Doestoevky-inspired, bohemian, peasant life. But neither meeting the Millers nor undergoing psychoanalysis were directly responsible for Nin's changing sense of self. Rather than accept Allendy's suggestion that she had only one true self to express in her dress and appearance, Nin embraced her "variegated" nature and life as "a woman with a hundred faces" (Diary 36, p. 27).

Implications: Composing a Text, Composing a Self

Scholars of life writing have written that as an author composes an autobiographical text, such as a diary, autobiography, or novel, the writer's self is composed as well (cf., Friedman, 1988). Susan Stanford Friedman (1988) included the following classics in her examples from nineteenth- and twentieth-century women's literature: Charlotte Perkins Gilman's *The Yellow Wallpaper*, H.D.'s *Hermione*, Gertrude Stein's *The Autobiography of Alice. B. Toklas* and Audre Lorde's *Zami: A New Spelling of My Name*. Friedman wrote, in discussing the above texts, that "women's autobiography comes alive as a literary tradition of self-creation" (Friedman, 1988, p. 55). Given the status of those texts referenced above, it is clear that there was indeed a literary tradition that was on its way to becoming well-established by the time Nin (1966) was first published. There is a stepping back that takes place as an author composes an autobiographical text, a "consideration of the formal structure" (Podnieks, 2000, pp. 4-5) that Culley (1985) marks as part of the "construction of self" that begins to take place as a diary is composed (Culley, 1985, p. 10).

> The act of autobiographical writing, particularly that which occurs in a periodic structure [such as a diary], involves the writer in complex literary as well as psychological processes. It is a paradox that the process whose frequent goal is to establish self-continuity involves at its heart a dislocation from the self, or a turning of subject into object....[T]he self stands apart to view the self. (Culley, 1985, p. 10)

For Nin, her construction of self had begun to take place as she wrote in her diary years before the period addressed by this study. As a teenager, modeling for artists and physically on display for long periods of time, Nin used her diary as a refuge and to give another side of herself a voice:

> ...she went without lunch to write in the diaries because she was modeling fifteen hours a day. In them, she poured out a self she couldn't let herself show to the world, the Anaïs who was something other than always gay, giving and all-healing. Her shadow self. (Stocking, 1971/1994, p. 100)

It is this construction of self that made Nin (1986) and her diaries ideal texts for analysis, given the turning points Nin was experiencing in her life when the diary entries were composed. At the opening of Nin (1986) and Diary 32, she had just returned from a pivotal trip to visit friends and family in New York (Nin, 1985). It was a trip she had dreaded, to the point that she had contemplated suicide by jumping off the ship on the voyage over (Nin, 1985, p. 469). The Nin who had just returned home to Louveciennes, France at the opening of Nin (1986) and Diary 32 was a very different woman from the one who sailed to New York, and her choice of title for the journal she finished right after that trip reflected that: "The Woman Who Died. Disintegration" (title page, Diary 31).

Written with Nin's well-practiced hand, combined with her own unique aesthetic sense, and inspired by the diaries and fiction she had read, the raw material of her unedited words in her handwritten diaries, from 1931 and 1932, therefore lent themselves well to being transformed into the hybrid diary/autobiographical novel, *Henry and June* (Nin, 1986). As noted before, Nin (1986) was edited posthumously by other hands (as explained in Chapter Three) and may be more aptly called an autobiographical novel. As far as factuality goes, as Gunther Stuhlmann, Nin's editor at Harcourt Brace Jovanovich wrote in his preface to the first volume of the diary (Nin, 1966), when describing the process of omitting persons or changing names before publication, "…as any reader will soon see, the factual identity of a person is basically important within the context of the diary. Miss Nin's truth, as we have seen, is psychological" (Nin, 1966, p. *xi*). In other words, the truth is subjective. On the subject of truth and literary form in American women's diaries from the eighteenth through the twentieth centuries, Culley (1985) wrote that diaries,

> [a]s invaluable as women's life-records…as historical sources [contain] a kind of "truth" about women's lives not found in other places…The process of selection and arrangement of detail in the text raises an array of concerns appropriately "literary," including questions of audience (real or implied), narrative, shape and structure, persona, [and] voice… (Culley, 1985, p. 10)

Gunther Stuhlmann (and, by extension, Nin) would probably have supported the conclusion, based on the argument above, that Nin's published diaries can be said to "contain a kind of truth not found in other places."

Limitations

This study was limited in that it examined just one twelve-month period in Nin's life (1931-1932). As such, it represents a snapshot in the life of Nin and her relationship with clothing. Second, there were few photographs of Nin available from this time period. Were new photographs to surface, an understanding of Nin's dress in the years 1931-1932 would be enhanced.

Suggestions for Future Study

Many potential topics for future research were touched on in Chapter Four, namely the details of Nin's *Maja* Spanish dance costume, her body image as it related to sense of self, and her performing of roles in different social contexts and for varying reasons. Nin's liking for Russian and "Byzantine" style is another topic for future research, as is her discussion of her "hundred faces."

Nin's published works of fiction contain many mentions of dress and the lives of the characters Djuna and Hans in *The Winter of Artifice* (Nin, 1939) were clearly based on Nin and Henry Miller's experiences as recorded in Nin's diaries (Diaries 32-36). Some of the descriptions of Djuna's dress in Nin (1939), based on text from the diaries, contain more detail than the original entries in the diaries, inviting speculation as to whether the added details were fiction or simply details that had been left out of the diary entries.

Potential for creative scholarship on this study's topic abounds. Recreations of Nin's dress as she described it in the diary could be used to enhance understanding of Nin's experience and appearance. Finally, given the amount of detail on dress and appearance that appeared in the sample of diaries that this study examined, and which other scholars have already identified (Krizan, 2011), it is likely that Nin's diaries contain a lifetime of reflections on her dress and appearance.

Conclusions

At one time, Nin's diaries were her publisher's top selling title on college and university campuses (Eckman, 1972/1994, p. 177). Over twenty years have elapsed since the tell-all biographies and the first unexpurgated diaries (Nin, 1986 & 1992) were released. Doyle (2015) sums up the perspective of the latest generation of Nin fans, who embrace Nin's life and style wholeheartedly:

> Nin, who was once called a 'narcissist' for gadding about in eye-catching thrift-shop costumes and dramatic makeup…the day-to-day work of celebrities, would have been at home in 2015. (Doyle, 2015, para. 36)

Anaïs Nin, at the ages of 28 and 29, on the heels of, and in the middle of, a few major turning points in life, was also in search of an identity when she wrote the material contained in the *Henry and June* (Nin, 1986) diaries. Dress scholar Tove Hermanson (2010) characterized Nin's identity in this time period as "fractured," something which was visible in her "sartorial selections" (Hermanson, 2010, para. 2). Kaiser (2012) wrote, in the context of appearances, that individuals are constantly undergoing a process of exploring who they are and who they are becoming (Kaiser, 2012, p. 30). Nin's search for, and construction of, her individual self in her diaries was part of her process of exploring who she was and who she was becoming.

Although initially uncertain about the value of the diaries as sources for historical truth, due to their portrayal in Bair (1995), examination of the diaries in UCLA, the Nin papers in USF, and Nin (1986), made clear that the diaries were essential in answering this study's research question: What was Nin's subjective experience of dress and appearance as described in her handwritten journals from October 1931-October 1932?

> Part of the seductiveness of writing a life is that it fosters the fantasy of perfect understanding. You start by imagining your subject as misunderstood and unappreciated, someone in need of rescue. Then you convince yourself that you are the first to recognize her, to see fully who she was....The more misunderstood the subject, the more intense her biographer's pleasure in slowly removing each veil. (Hornstein, 1994, p. 53)

Echoing Hornstein's (1994) words above, this study began with the intent to write Nin's life by documenting her dress and appearance as expressed in her diaries from October 1931 – October 1932. However, as the quotes from the discussion of Nin's dress in the 1960s and 1970s in Chapter Two and this study's data from the 1930s revealed, Nin's appearance was not "unappreciated" by those who knew her in life. Nin's self-reflexivity and awareness of her appearance and its appraisal by others were described in her journals at length. This study's purpose, to discover Anaïs Nin's expression of her dress and appearance, as communicated in her handwritten journals from October 1931 through October 1932, has been fulfilled. Furthermore, this study's findings underscored the value of diaries as sources of information in the study of dress history and the subjective experience of appearance.

References

Adler, S. (1980). A diary and a dress. *Dress, 6*(1), 83-88. doi: 10.1179/036121180805298664

Bair, D. (1995). *Anaïs Nin: A biography*. New York, NY: Penguin Books.

Bald, W. (1987). *On the left bank: 1929-1933*. Athens, OH: Ohio University Press.

Bartky, S. L. (1997). Foucault, femininity, and the modernization of patriarchal power. In Diana Tietjens Meyers (Ed.). *Feminist social thought: A reader*, (93-111). New York, NY: Routledge.

Basenotes. (n.d.). Reviews of Narcisse Noir by Caron. [Web page]. Retrieved January 24, 2017, from http://www.basenotes.net/fragrancereviews/fragrance/10210551

Baumgarten, L. (1996). Dressing for pregnancy: A maternity gown of 1780–1795. *Dress, 23*(1), 16-24. doi: 10.1179/036121196805298045

Blodgett, H. (1996). Preserving the moment in the diary of Margaret Fountaine. In *Inscribing the Daily: Critical essays on women's diaries*. In S.L. Bunkers and C.A. Huff, (Eds.), pp. 156-168. Amherst, Massachusetts: University of Massachusetts Press.

Bonney, T., & Bonney, L. (1929). *A shopping guide to Paris*. New York, NY: Robert McBride & Company.

Bordo, S. (2003). *Unbearable weight: Feminism, western culture, and the body*. Berkeley, CA: University of California Press.

Butler, J. (1997). Performative acts and gender constitution: An essay in phenomenology and feminist theory. In K. Conboy, N. Medina, & S. Stanbury, (Eds.), *Writing on the body: Female embodiment and feminist theory*, (pp. 401-417). New York, NY: Columbia University Press.

_____. (2007). *Gender trouble: Feminism and the subversion of identity*. New York, NY: Routledge.

Cross, R. (1991). *Henry Miller: The Paris years*. Big Sur, CA: Peeramid Press.

Culley, M. (1985). *A day at a time: The diary literature of American women from 1764 to the present*. New York, NY: The Feminist Press at the City University of New York.

Davis, K. (1999). Cosmetic surgery in a different voice: The case of Madame Noël. *Women's Studies International Forum, 22*(5), 473–488. doi: 10.1016/S0277-5395(99)00052-7

Dearborn, M. V. (1991). *The happiest man alive: A biography of Henry Miller*. New York, NY: Simon and Schuster.

Dick, K. C. (1967). *Henry Miller: Colossus of one*. Sittard, The Netherlands: Alberts.

Doyle, S. (7 April, 2015). "Before Lena Dunham, there was Anaïs Nin - now patron saint of social media." *The Guardian*. Retrieved February 1, 2016, from http://www.theguardian.com/culture/2015/apr/07/anais-nin-author-social-media

Duxler, M. B. (2002). *Seduction: A portrait of Anaïs Nin*. Boulder, Colorado: EdgeWork Books.

Eckman, F. M. (1972/1994). The non-legend of Anaïs Nin. In W. M. DuBow (Ed.), *Conversations with Anaïs Nin*, (pp. 172-177). Jackson, Mississippi: University of Mississippi.

Faucheux, A. (2016) Anaïs, Henry, and June: Reading nonmonogamy in literature. *Journal of Bisexuality, 16*(3), 294-311. doi: 10.1080/15299716.2016.1195782

Fitch, N. R. (1993). *Anaïs Nin: The erotic life of Anaïs Nin*. Boston, MA: Back Bay Books/Little, Brown and Company.

Fitzpatrick, M. L. (2007). Historical research: The method." In P. L. Munhall, (Ed.), *Nursing research: A qualitative perspective*, (pp. 404-415). Boston, Massachusetts: Jones and Bartlett Publishers.

Foucault, M. (1975/1977). *Discipline and punish: The birth of the prison*. Trans. Alan Sheridan. New York, NY: Vintage Books/Random House.

Fragrantica. (n.d.). Narcisse Noir Caron perfume a fragrance for women 1911. [Web page]. Retrieved January 24, 2017, from http://www.fragrantica.com/perfume/Caron/NarcisseNoir5593.html

Friedman, S. S. (1988). Women's autobiographical selves: Theory and practice. In S. Benstock, (Ed.), *The private self: Theory and practice of women's autobiographical writings*, (pp. 34-62). Chapel Hill, NC: The University of North Carolina Press.

Freud, S. (1933/1961). *New introductory lectures on psycho-analysis*. Trans. Peter Strachey (Ed.). New York, NY: W.W. Norton and Company.

Glaser, B. G., & Strauss, A. L. (1967). *The discovery of grounded theory: Strategies for qualitative research*. Chicago: Aldine Publishing Company.

Goffman, E. (1959). *The presentation of self in everyday life*. New York, NY: Anchor Books.

Gordon, B. (1987). Textiles and clothing in the Civil War: A portrait for contemporary understanding. *Clothing and Textiles Research Journal, 5*(3), 41-47.

_____. (1992). Meanings in mid-nineteenth century dress: Images from New England women's writings. *Clothing and Textiles Research Journal, 10*(3), 44-53.

Hermanson, T. (2010, September 29). "The deforming mirror: Anaïs Nin's fractured identity as read through fashion." [Blog post]. Thread for Thought. http://www.threadforthought.net/deforming-mirror-anais-nins-fractured-identity-read-fashion/ Accessed April 28, 2017.

Herron, P. (1996). *Anaïs Nin: A book of mirrors*. Huntington Woods, Michigan: Sky Blue Press.

Herron, P., & Bair, D. (2010). The making of *Anaïs Nin: A biography*: Paul Herron interviews Deirdre Bair. *A Café in Space, 7*, 27-34.

Hillestad, R. (1980). The underlying structures of appearance. *Dress, 6*(1), 117-125.

Hornstein, G. A. (1994). The ethics of ambiguity: Feminists writing women's lives. In C. E. Franz, & A. J. Stewart, (Eds.), *Women creating lives: Identities, resilience, and resistance*, (pp. 51-68). Boulder, CO: Westview Press.

Hughes, C. (2005). *Dressed in fiction*. Oxforg: Berg.

Jacob, J., & Cerny, C. (2004). Radical drag appearances and identity: The embodiment of male femininity and social critique. *Clothing and Textiles Research Journal, 22*(3), 122-134.

Jarczok, A. (2017). *Writing an icon: Celebrity culture and the invention of Anaïs Nin.* Athens, Ohio: Swallow Press/Ohio University Press.

Jelinek, E. (1974, Dec 31). Anaïs reconsidered. *Off Our Backs, 4*(12), 18-19.

Jong, E. (1994). *The devil at large: Erica Jong on Henry Miller.* New York, NY: Grove Press.

Kadar, M. (1992). Coming to terms: Life writing—from genre to critical practice. In M. Kadar (Ed.), *Essays on life writing: From genre to critical practice*, (pp. 3-16). Toronto: University of Toronto Press.

Kaiser, S. B. (2012). *Fashion and cultural studies.* London: Bloomsbury.

Kraft, B. (2013). *Anaïs Nin: The last days, a memoir.* San Jose, CA: Pegasus Books.

_____. (2016). Henry Miller: The last days: An excerpt from the new memoir. *A Café in Space: The Anaïs Nin Literary Journal, 13*, 21-29.

Krizan, K. (2011). Anaïs style: The birth of a lifelong passion. *A Café in Space: The Anaïs Literary Journal, 8*, 111-119.

Lejeune, P. (1989). The autobiographical pact. In P.J. Eakan (Ed.). *On autobiography*, (pp. 3-30). Trans. Katherine Leary. Minneapolis, MN: Minnesota University Press.

Lejeune, P. (2009). *On diary.* In J. D. Popkin & J. Rak, (Eds.). Trans. Katherine Durnin. Manoa, Hawai'i: University of Hawai'i Press.

Mallon, T. (1984). *A book of one's own: People and their diaries.* New York, NY: Ticknor & Fields.

Marcketti, S. B., & Angstman, E. T. (2013). The trend for mannish suits in the 1930s. *Dress, 39*(2), 135-152.

Marcketti, S. B., & Parsons, J. L. (2016). *Knock it off! A history of design piracy in women's ready-to-wear industry.* Lubbock, TX: Texas Tech University Press.

McNeil, P., Karaminas, V., & Cole, C. (2009). Introduction: Fashion in fiction: Text and clothing in literature, film, and television. In P. McNeil, V. Karaminas, & Cole, C. (Eds.), *Fashion in Fiction* (pp. 1-8). Oxford: Berg.

Merriam S. B. (2009). *Qualitative research: A guide to design and implementation*. San Francisco, CA: Jossey-Bass.

Merriam, S. B., & Tisdell, E. J. (2016). *Qualitative research: A guide to design and implementation*. San Francisco, CA: Jossey-Bass.

Miller, H. (1934/1961). *Tropic of cancer*. New York, NY: Grove Press.

Moon, C. E., & Ogle, J. P. (2013). The "hybrid hero" in Western dime novels: An analysis of women's gender performance, dress, and identity in the Deadwood Dick series. *Clothing and Textiles Research Journal, 31*(2), 109-124.

Mun, J. M., Janigo, K. A., & Johnson, K. K. P. (2012). Tattoo and the self. *Clothing and Textiles Research Journal, 30*(2), 134-148.

Nalbantian, S. (1997). Aesthetic lies. In S. Nalbantian, (Ed.), *Anaïs Nin: Literary perspectives*, (pp. 3-22). New York, NY: St. Martin's Press.

Nin, A. (1932). *D. H. Lawrence: An unprofessional study*. Paris: Edward W. Titus.

_____. (1936). *The house of incest*. Paris: Siana Editions.

_____. (1939). *The winter of artifice*. Paris: The Obelisk Press.

_____. (1959/1987). *Cities of the interior*. Athens, Ohio: Swallow Press/Ohio University Press.

_____. (1966). *The diary of Anaïs Nin, volume 1: 1931-1934*. San Diego, CA: Harvest/The Swallow Press & Harcourt, Inc.

_____. (1967). *The diary of Anaïs Nin, volume 2: 1934-1939*. San Diego, CA: Harvest/The Swallow Press & Harcourt Brace & Company.

_____. (1968). *The novel of the future*. New York, NY: The MacMillan Company.

_____. (1969). *The diary of Anaïs Nin, volume 3: 1939-1944*. New York, NY:

Harvest/Harcourt Brace Jovanovich, Inc.

———. (1976). *In favor of the sensitive man and other essays*. New York, NY: Harvest/Harcourt Brace Jovanovich.

———. (1977). *Delta of Venus: Erotica*. San Diego, CA: Harcourt Brace Jovanovich, Publishers.

———. (1978). *Linotte: The early diary of Anaïs Nin, volume 1: 1914-1920*. San Diego, CA: Harcourt, Brace & Company.

———. (1979). *Little birds*. San Diego, CA: Harcourt, Brace & Company.

———. (1982). *The early diary of Anaïs Nin, volume 2: 1920-1923*. San Diego, CA: Harcourt Brace Jovanovich, Publishers.

———. (1983). *The early diary of Anaïs Nin, volume 3: 1923-1927*. San Diego, CA: Harvest/Harcourt Brace Jovanovich.

———. (1985). *The early diary of Anaïs Nin, volume 4: 1927-1931*. San Diego, CA: Harvest/Harcourt Brace Jovanovich.

———. (1986). *Henry & June, from a journal of love: The unexpurgated diary of Anaïs Nin, 1931-1932*. Orlando, FL: Harcourt, Inc.

———. (1992). *Incest, from a journal of love: The unexpurgated diary of Anaïs Nin,1932-1934*. San Diego, CA: Harvest/Harcourt, Brace & Company.

———. (1995). *Fire, from a journal of love: The unexpurgated diary of Anaïs Nin, 1934-1937*. San Diego, CA: Harvest/Harcourt, Inc.

———. (2017). *Trapeze: The unexpurgated diary of Anaïs Nin: 1947-1955*. San Antonio, TX: Sky Blue Press/Ohio University Press.

Nussbaum, F. A. (1988). Toward conceptualizing diary. In J. Olney, (Ed.), *Studies in autobiography*, (pp. 128-140). New York, NY: Oxford University Press.

Podnieks, E. (2000). *Daily modernism: The literary diaries of Virginia Woolf, Antonia White, Elizabeth Smart, and Anaïs Nin*. Montreal: McGill-Queen's University Press.

Pole, R., & Ferrone, J. (2007) The making of *Henry and June*, the book:

Correspondence 1985-1986. *A Café in Space: The Anaïs Nin Literary Journal, 4,* 8-21.

Rabine, L. W. (2007). Flora Tristan's closet. *The Romanic Review, 98*(1), 51-69.

Raphael, M. (2003). *Anais Nin: The voyage within: A biographical novel.* Lincoln, Nebraska: iUniverse, Inc.

Rivière, J. (1929). Womanliness as a masquerade. *The International Journal of Psycho-Analysis, 10,* 303-313.

Roach-Higgins, M. E., & Eicher, J. B. (1992). Dress and identity. *Clothing and Textiles Research Journal, 10*(4), 1-8.

Sanders, E. (2011). Female slave narratives and appearance: Assimilation, experience, and escape. *Clothing and Textiles Research Journal, 29*(4), 267-283.

Saville, D. (2003). Freud, flappers and bohemians: The influence of modern psychological thought and social ideology on dress, 1910–1923. *Dress, 30*(1), 63-79. doi: 10.1179/036121103805253244

Steele, V. (1998). Proust's world of fashion. In V. Steele, *Paris fashion: A cultural history,* (pp. 193-217). Oxford: Berg.

Stocking, S. (1971/1994). Personas unmasked in visit with Anaïs Nin. In Wendy M. DuBow (Ed.), *Conversations with Anaïs Nin,* (pp. 98-103). Jackson, Miss: University Press of Mississippi.

Tookey, H. (2003). *Anaïs Nin, fictionality and femininity: Playing a thousand roles.* Oxford: Oxford University.

Tortora, P. G. & Marcketti, S. B. (2015). *Survey of historic costume, 6th edition.* New York, NY: Fairchild Books.

Tseëlon, E. (1997). *The masque of femininity: The presentation of woman in everyday life.* London: Sage Publications.

Tseëlon, E., & Kaiser, S. B. (1992). A dialogue with feminist film theory: Multiple readings of the gaze. *Studies in Symbolic Interaction, 13,* 119-137.

Tyner, K.E., & Ogle, J.P. (2009). Feminist theory of the dressed body: A comparative analysis and applications for textiles and clothing scholarship. *Clothing and Textiles Research Journal, 27*(2), 98-121.

Van Cleave, K. (2005). "A style all her own": Fashion, clothing practices, and female community at Smith College, 1920–1929. *Dress, 32*(1), 56-65. doi: 10.1179/036121105805253044

Vaughan, H. A. (2006). Natacha Rambova: Fashion designer (1928–1931). *Dress, 33*(1), 21-39. doi: 10.1179/036121106805252972

Wrisley, M. (2006). Stella Blum grant report: "Fashion I despised": Charlotte Perkins Gilman and American dress reform, 1880–1920. *Dress, 33*(1), 97-110. doi: 10.1179/036121106805253025

www.ingramcontent.com/pod-product-compliance
Lightning Source LLC
Chambersburg PA
CBHW030345240426
43661CB00052B/1749